SOUTH YORKSHIRE SUPERTRAM
Britain's First Modern Tramway

by Peter Fox

BACKGROUND

Sheffield was the last city in England to dispense with trams, operation ceasing on 8th October 1960 when the route from Vulcan Road (Tinsley) to Beauchief succumbed to the bus. Sheffield's old trams were all four-wheelers, bogie cars having been ruled-out because of the need to operate over fierce gradients in this city which, like Rome, is built on seven hills. As a result, the Sheffield cars tended to pitch at speed, but in spite of this, Sheffielders tend to regard the first tramway era with affection, and it must be said that the 1936 'domed-roof' design looked strikingly modern for its time. Sheffield cars had 2 + 1 seating and were therefore more comfortable than the buses which replaced them.

The first suggestion that trams might return to Sheffield was made in 1974, when a network of modern tram routes was one of the options considered by the Sheffield and Rotherham land-use transportation study which was undertaken by Alan Voorhees and Associates (now known as MVA Consultancy). Later, tram routes were incorporated into one of the more detailed options for evaluation, but despite the fact that this option seemed attractive, the chosen option was more conventional in its approach.

THE PRESENT SCHEME

The present scheme originated in 1985, when the South Yorkshire Passenger Transport Executive (the PTE) put forward a proposal for a light rail route from Hillsborough (Middlewood) to Mosborough, with branches from Stannington and to Herdings. The Stannington route was later cut back to Malin Bridge following opposition from local residents, aided and abetted by the leader of the Sheffield Liberals, who has since consistently helped to organise opposition to the whole scheme, despite the fact that the Liberal Party's national transport policy is in favour of light rail.

The scheme eventually gained support from the ruling Labour group on the City Council, providing that a second route was developed to help regenerate Sheffield's east end, an area devastated by the closure of most of the city's steelworks. The Council also wanted the depot resited from its original position at Halfway to a site on the second route. Accordingly, a scheme for line 2 was developed from the new shopping and leisure complex at Meadowhall to a triangular junction with line 1 at Park Square. Full details of the various parliamentary bills and their progress were detailed in 'Light Rail Review 1' and are updated in 'Light Rail Developments in the UK', elsewhere in this publication.

It was hoped to start work on line 2 in 1990, so that a section would be ready for the World Student Games in July 1991, but unfortunately Government funding was held back, despite the scheme satisfying the criteria for grant, until December 1990, when the Minister for Public Transport, Roger Freeman, announced that the Government had approved a 50% section 56 grant for the scheme. The remaining 50% would be accounted for by credit approval to the local authorities which finance the PTE, with the Government providing increased support to these authorities to service the loan. There will also be contributions from the developers of Meadowhall, the Sheffield Development Corporation and Sheffield City Council.

Mr. Freeman gave four reasons for the award of funding:

- The benefits to non-users.
- Reduction of congestion.
- Impact on regeneration.
- Improvement of the environment.

▲ The mock-up of the Sheffield LRV outside Sheffield Cathedral on 12th December 1990.
Peter Fox

▶ Access for mothers with pushchairs could not be easier in this low-floor-entrance vehicle, to the delight of this lady.
Peter Fox

ORGANISATION

The Supertram scheme was conceived by the PTE. In order to put the scheme on the same footing as other local transport, a wholly-owned subsidiary company known as South Yorkshire Supertram Ltd. (SYSL) has been created. SYSL is responsible to its client, the PTE, for the design, building and operation of the system. Its only asset is its concession. It has eight directors, three from the PTE, four from private industry (Davy-McKee, Midland Bank, Pannel-Kerr-Forster and Presto Tools) and the Chief Executive of SYSL. The PTE is the owner of the vehicles and infrastructure and retains full technical control over the whole system. Incidentally Messrs Pannel-Kerr-Forster were originally objectors to the scheme! The directors will be required to make an operating profit. As a condition of granting finance for the scheme, the present government requires that the system be eventually sold to the private sector.

The various activities associated with the running of the system which will be sub-contracted are as follows:

● Operation of the system.
● Maintenance of the rolling stock.
● Maintenance of Civil Engineering structures and buildings.
● Maintenance of platforms, shelters and lighting.
● Maintenance of track.
● Maintenance of signalling and telecommunications.
● Maintenance of power supply and distribution including overhead line equipment.
● Maintenance of landscaping.

PREPARATION AND DESIGN OF THE SCHEME

The preparation of the scheme up to the stage of parliamentary approval and the preparation of the submission to the government for funding required much preliminary work in the shape of public consultation and studies in the fields of engineering, architecture, financial evaluation etc.

Public consultation was undertaken at various stages in the process by Sheffield City Council, both on a local basis in areas affected by the scheme and in the form of a city centre display where the general public were asked to comment on the scheme.

In order to satisfy the rigorous criteria demanded by the Department of Transport for availability of grant, an economic evaluation had to be produced which took account of traffic forecasts, effect on modal split and in particular the quantification of non-user benefits, i.e. the time benefits to non-users, particularly motorists, brought about by the transfer of car-users to Supertram. This was carried out by MVA Consultancy. A further study relating to employment and land-use opportunities was carried out by the Barton Willmore Partnership (who also conducted a similar study for the Docklands Light Railway).

Other companies which have been involved previously include Turner and Townsend Quantity Surveyors, Kennedy Henderson Ltd. and the John Brunton Partnership (architects).

Further public consultation will be undertaken by the Frank Graham Group, in particular to discuss with frontagers details regarding such matters as car parking. There will also be further exhibitions and public meetings and groups representing special interests will also be consulted. It is hoped to find a permanent site for the vehicle mock-up, and this could possibly be at Sheffield Transport Interchange or Meadowhall Interchange.

Main contractors for the scheme are:
● **Siemens plc:** Rolling stock.
● **Balfour Beatty Power Ltd.:** Track, structures, traffic control and ticketing.

Detailed design of the scheme is being undertaken by the following constractors:
● **Design & Building Services (Sheffield City Council):** Structures, design work, highway engineering, civil supervision and traffic management.
● **Turner and Townsend Quantity Surveyors:** Payment, valuations, contractual and cost advice etc.
● **Kennedy-Henderson:** Design approval, rolling stock supervision, M & E supervision.
● **John Brunton Partnership:** Architecture and landscape architecture.

The whole scheme is being supervised by **Turner & Townsend Project Management Ltd.**, who are acting independantly of the contractors.

THE SYSTEM

Whilst the Manchester system is basically a piece of tramway connecting two existing ex-BR routes (hence the name 'Metrolink'), the South Yorkshire scheme is the United Kingdom's first completely new street-based LRT system. Line 1 is completely new in its entirety and line 2 only follows a railway alignment for part of its length. The cost at around £230 million makes the scheme the largest public transport investment project in real terms outside London since the Tyne & Wear Metro was built.

Whereas the Manchester system, because of its use of ex-BR lines with high-platform stations is basically a high-platform system, the South Yorkshire system is a low-platform system with low-floor entrances in the cars. Thus the name 'South Yorkshire Supertram' was chosen as the most appropriate name. Incidentally, although the lines under construction are basically in Sheffield, around 150 route-metres are in Rotherham and 972 route-metres are in North-East Derbyshire! All stations are in Sheffield.

THE LRVs

The choice of low platforms, together with the desirability of meeting the needs of the mobility-impaired, implied the selection of an LRV with low-floor entrances. It was not possible to have a vehicle of the Grenoble-type because of the necessity of having all axles powered.

The chosen design is supplied by Siemens-Duewag of Düsseldorf, Germany, a similar design by Asea-Brown Boveri having been rejected. Also considered was the all-low-floor MAN vehicle, which was offered by GEC-Alsthom, but the PTE did not like the layout of this experimental vehicle. There will be 25 cars, the total cost of these including spares being approximately £42 million.

The design is an eight axle, double-ended, double-articulated car, around 35 m long and 2.65 m wide and seats 100 passengers, with room for 150 standing at 4 per m^2. The weight of the all-steel vehicle is expected to be around 44.5 tonnes and the maximum speed is 80 km/h (50 mph). High quality finishes will aim to discourage vandalism and will be easy to repair or replace.

The four bogies each have a DC monomotor, each driving both axles of the bogie through flexible couplings. The one-hour rating of these is 277 kW each, but they may be de-rated to 250 kW. Bochum 84 resilient wheels are fitted. The layout

▲The cab interior of the LRV is very stylish.   *MEDA*

▼An artist's impression of the proposed bridge over the Sheffield Canal.   *John Brunton Partnership/David Carter*

SOUTH YORKSHIRE
SUPERTRAM

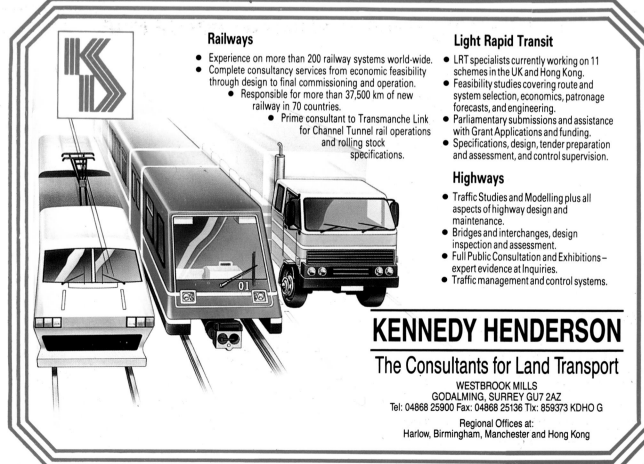

of the vehicle can be seen from the photograph of the model. The low-level floor area between the doors, which are situated in the end body-sections only is 420 mm high at the doors, sloping up to 450 mm in the centre of the car. It will be laid out to suit the mobility-impaired and passengers with luggage, push-chairs etc. The higher floor areas situated behind the cabs and in the centre body section are 880 mm high and are reached by only two steps and will contain comfortable seating. Tinted windows with hopper ventilators are provided to reduce glare. Heating is by fan-assisted convectors and destination indicators outside will be of the motorised-blind type. Inside there will be dot-matrix indicators which might be used to denote the next stop.

Control is by GTO choppers which give stepless control of traction and braking, the main service brake being regenerative. There are also air-operated disc brakes on each axle and magnetic track brakes on each bogie. Sanding is provided on all axles to improve adhesion when necessary. Most of the control equipment is mounted on the roof of each outer body section, whilst auxillary equipment such as batteries, air compressor and static convertors are located under the floor of the centre body. Extensive fault monitoring facilities will be available within the control equipment to pinpoint faults when they do happen and ease maintenance and rectification work. A data-recording facility is also provided. On-board equipment will also identify the tram to the special lineside tramway signals, coordinated where appropriate with the normal road

▲The model of the Supertram. Note that the articulations are not over the bogies, owing to all axles being powered. Almost all seats are facing and line up with the windows. BR please take note!
Peter Fox

▼The interior of the mock-up, showing different types of seats. The ones on the left were liked by most visitors. *MEDA*

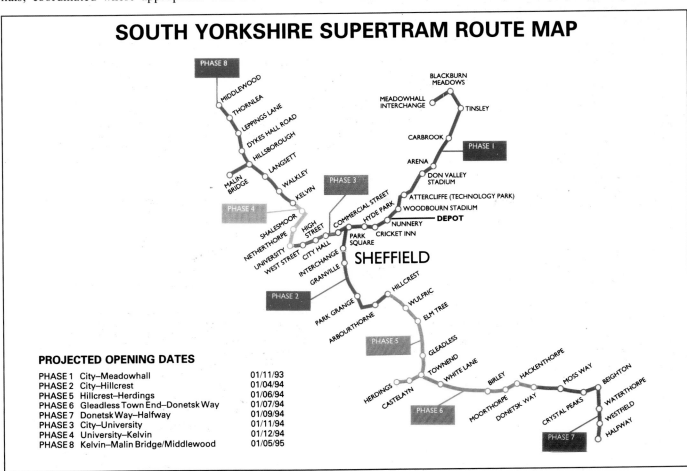

SOUTH YORKSHIRE SUPERTRAM ROUTE MAP

PROJECTED OPENING DATES

PHASE 1	City–Meadowhall	01/11/93
PHASE 2	City–Hillcrest	01/04/94
PHASE 5	Hillcrest–Herdings	01/06/94
PHASE 6	Gleadless Town End–Donetsk Way	01/07/94
PHASE 7	Donetsk Way–Halfway	01/09/94
PHASE 3	City–University	01/11/94
PHASE 4	University–Kelvin	01/12/94
PHASE 8	Kelvin–Malin Bridge/Middlewood	01/05/95

traffic lights, to give priority as far as possible to Supertram when operating in mixed traffic or through junctions. External lighting will be very similar to other road vehicles but will identify Supertrams specially to other road users.

LINE 1. MIDDLEWOOD/MALIN BRIDGE–HALFWAY/HERDINGS

Line 1 starts at Middlewood on the north-western outskirts of Sheffield, the route following the previous Middlewood tram route as far as Shalesmoor. Alignment on this section will mainly be in the carriageway, but there is an opportunity to run at the side of the road on reservation just before Kelvin. It should be noted that the parallel Penistone Road is being converted to a dual carriageway so that most of the Supertram route will be downgraded to public transport and access only. The short Malin Bridge branch joins at Hillsborough Corner, where there is a prosperous suburban shopping area. This branch is entirely on-street. At its terminus a one-way traffic system is followed to form a loop and hence there is no need for reversal, although there is also the option of operating to a stub terminus on private land. Malin Bridge is the gateway to the beautiful Rivelin Valley.

At Shalesmoor the route deviates from the former tram route to run on the centre reservation of the Inner Ring Road to the University, where there will be the Brook Hill Underpass which will run under a roundabout. The route then swings east along Glossop Road, West Street and Church Street (which were previously on the old Crookes and Walkley tram routes), to the city centre in High Street and Commercial Street. Again the roads concerned are routes which are not used for through motor traffic.

Commercial Street is at present a dual carriageway which leads onto an enormous round traffic island called 'Park Square'. This is probably the most important road junction in Sheffield, as it is the end of the Sheffield Parkway, the main route into Sheffield from the M1 motorway. Clearly the LRT route has to be segregated at this point, and the solution has been to use the eastbound lane of Commercial Street as the tramway. At the bottom, a 70 metre span bowstring arch bridge leads to the island where the line turns sharp right over a single-span concrete bridge to run along Granville Street at an upper level parallel to the Midland station. A station will be built here and will be connected both to the new Transport Interchange (bus station) and to the Midland Railway station. The details of how this will be achieved have not yet been finalised.

Past Granville, the line starts to climb, helped by the Norfolk Park Road Viaduct, needed because the ruling 1 in 10 gradient would be exceeded without it and also because the road junction at that spot is complicated. The gradient along the viaduct is 1 in 20, but the climb up Park Grange Road on the Norfolk Park Estate soon gets steeper so that around 400 metres of the route are at 1 in 12. The parliamentary submission for this section of the line had one reserved track on each side of the carriageway, but the actual alignment is not yet decided. Park Grange Road curves to the east and levels out and just past Hillcrest, the route turns south to run up City Road to Elm Tree. This section formed part of the old Intake tram route. Originally, the new tramway was to have run through the Manor Estate, when it was thought that the area was to be redeveloped, but there was a change of plan by the City Council in favour of refurbishment of existing properties. This meant that the opportunity of a new reserved track route was lost, and since the existing road layout was unsuitable, the decision was taken to run up City Road.

At Elm Tree, the route turns south along the outer ring road, alignment generally being along the central reservation of the dual carriageway. At Gleadless Town End, the main line turns east down White Lane, whilst the Herdings branch carries straight on for a short distance along the central reservation as a single line, eventually bearing west and leaving the

road alignment to run through open space for around 600 m to a terminus at Raeburn Road. The highest point of the system is on this open space at 212.09 m (694 ft) above sea level, having climbed 143.65 m (471 ft) from the city centre.

The alignment along White Lane is on-street until the 'Old Harrow' public house is reached. Just past here is the county boundary. On entering Derbyshire, the line runs through fields for around 900 m, eventually running back into Sheffield on Birley Lane. Birley Moor Road is crossed and the line then starts to descend into an area which has been recently developed as a satellite township to Sheffield known collectively as Mosborough. The alignment from here onwards is virtually all on reservation, either alongside the roads or across fields.

The new shopping and leisure complex known as 'Crystal Peaks' has its own bus station, and the tram station will be adjacent to this. The terminus at Halfway is 69.67 m (228 ft) above sea level.

LINE 2. PARK SQUARE–MEADOWHALL INTERCHANGE

Line 2 starts with a triangular junction on the Park Square roundabout and heads east on a six-span post-tensioned reinforced concrete segmental viaduct which is 350 m long. Unlike Line 1, Line 2 has virtually no street-running. The viaduct runs along the south side of the Sheffield Parkway and then swings north to cross the road, turning east again and then north at Nunnery. A loop line leaves here on the northern side to serve the depot, which is built on the site of the former London & North Western Railway engine shed. After Nunnery, the alignment crosses the Great Central Railway line from Sheffield to Worksop and then runs along Woodbourn Road, initially on-street and then on reservation, in an area which has seen most of its old industry and all its slum housing demolished. The names of the next four stations all reflect the redevelopment of the area, Woodbourn Stadium being an existing sports stadium and Attercliffe Technology Park being a city council-sponsored development project, whilst the Don Valley Stadium and the Arena are both new projects developed for the World Student Games (Universiade).

At the end of Woodbourn Road, an interesting bridge takes the route over the Sheffield Canal. The design of this takes as its inspiration the bridge over the Ironbridge Gorge in Shropshire (the world's first iron bridge). Alongside Chippingham Street is Technology Park station and the line then continues along until the former Great Central Railway route from Sheffield to Doncaster via Rotherham Central is reached.

The only regular traffic along this line is three freight trips per day from Tinsley to the BSC works at Stocksbridge. It is also used by light engines and for diversionary use when the main ex-Midland Railway route from Sheffield to Rotherham is blocked by engineering work. A further occasional use is for football specials to Wadsley Bridge, the station near to the Sheffield Wednesday football ground at Hillsborough. This ground is, of course, also served by Supertram Line 1. Because of the requirement for a large number of sidings associated with the former steelworks along this route, the trackbed is quite wide, and there is room for three tracks, two SYSL and one BR. The LRT system follows this line as far as Tinsley South Junction, where it turns west, utilising the alignment of the former GCR Barnsley branch alongside the M1 Tinsley Viaduct. It then turns south-west to run alongside the main Sheffield–Rotherham railway line and terminates at the brand-new Meadowhall Interchange, adjacent to the Meadowhall shopping complex. This Interchange already consists of a 16-stand bus station and a four-platform railway station and cost £9.2 million.

The gradients on Line 2 are not as severe as Line 1. There are stretches of 1 in 20 in the Parkway–Nunnery area, plus a 150 metre stretch at 1 in 12.5 where the line crosses the railway and drops down onto Woodburn Road, but from Technology Park to Meadowhall Interchange the maximum gradient is 1 in 62 (almost level by LRT standards!)

INFRASTRUCTURE

Detailed design of the infrastructure has not yet been carried out, in particular as regards station design and the exact location and type of track. Each station will have a shelter, seats, lighting, display and ticketing equipment and will be designed to minimise vandalism. Some stations will consist of island platforms.

Track will be of three types:

● Ordinary railway rail to BS80A (80 lb/yd).
● Tramway rail to the French 35G-TF specification (55.23 kg/m).
● Switch and crossing rail to RI60.

Overhead line equipment will generally consist of twin contact wire either fixed to polymeric span-wire off adjacent buildings or suspended from masts affixed centrally between the tracks. Voltage will be 750 V dc.

Signalling to railway principles will be required for single-line sections and areas of restricted visibility and may or may not be fitted on the totally segregated sections of Line 2. If fitted, it would enable higher speeds to be achieved. It has not been decided whether such signals would be red/green, or whether they would consist of rows of white lights as will be used on the on-street sections where special signals for trams are required.

CONTROL AND OPERATION

The driver will have a radio link to central control and both the driver and central control will be able to give messages to passengers over the public address system. Surprisingly, no automatic vehicle monitoring is specified, but it should surely be possible, using the computer equipment on-board the cars to interrogate passive transponders in the track, and to automatically pass on the vehicle's position to a central computer using the same radio channel as for voice communication utilising a time-division multiplex system.

As well as the driver, a large number of revenue-protection staff will be employed, although it has not yet been decided whether or not there will be one per vehicle. There would be decided advantages in having a 'train captain' who could also look after the welfare of passengers. and act as a deterrent to prevent misdemeanour.

Normal services would operate at five-minute frequencies, giving a ten-minute frequency on each of the branches of Line 1. Exact journey times have not yet been calculated, but the following are estimates:

City Centre to Meadowhall 15 minutes
         Halfway   28 minutes
         Herdings   17 minutes
         Middlewood   20 minutes

TIMESCALE

Construction should start on 1st August 1991, with the first vehicle expected to arrive in the Spring of 1993, and nine are required for the opening of the first phase.

The BR track and signalling alterations on the Woodburn Jn.–Tinsley line are scheduled for Easter 1992 and immunisation of the signalling at Sheffield Midland against 750 V dc is scheduled for Easter 1993.

THE FUTURE

The obvious question which occurs to everyone is 'where will the next lines go?'. This is a question to which the PTE is addressing itself in a series of corridor studies in which many different modal options are being tested. The PTE is not only concerned with Sheffield and one corridor of great interest is that between Barnsley and Doncaster. LRT is being considered here, but it may be that heavy rail is more appropriate.

The most likely candidate for an extension to Supertram is the extension of Line 2 from Tinsley to Rotherham. This is only a short distance (3 km) and would have the benefit of connecting Rotherham to Sheffield by light rail, as well as providing a fast link between Rotherham and Meadowhall.

Another likely extension is along the Chesterfield Road/Abbeydale Road corridor. These roads serve suburbs of high car ownership and there exists the possibility of running alongside the BR Midland Main Line between Heeley and Millhouses, thereby providing fast transit times. Heavy rail and guided bus have also been proposed for this route, which is attracting a 'ribbon' development of business parks alongside the railway line, but the former would not provide adequate city centre penetration and the latter would provide little more than the bus lanes which already exist. The author's favourite option would be for an extension of Line 2 south-westwards along Arundel Gate and Bramall Lane, thence alongside the BR main line to Millhouses Park, crossing over to run alongside Abbeydale Road South and Baslow Road to Totley with a branch to Totley Brook and Dore.

The future is certainly rosy for Britain's first modern tramway and the author looks forward to being on one of the first trams to operate in 1993.

ACKNOWLEDGEMENTS

I would like to thank John Jordan of South Yorkshire PTE, Roger Jones of Kennedy Henderson and Chris Longley of South Yorkshire Supertram Ltd. for their help in the preparation of this feature.

◄An aeriel view of Sheffield City Centre, showing the route of Supertram. The new Olympic-standard Ponds Forge swimming pool can be seen above right of the triangle of lines.
Chorley & Handford Ltd.

▼A model of the bowstring arch bridge at the bottom of Commercial Street. *Peter Fox*

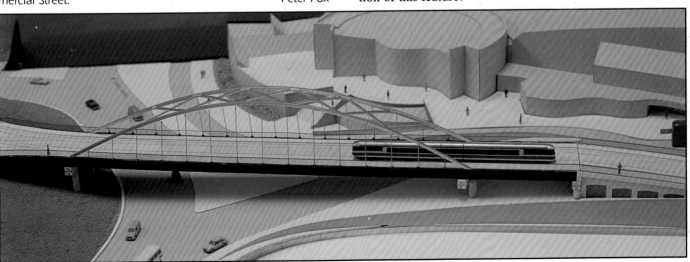

MODEL SYSTEM
Go to Grenoble!
by Michael Taplin, Chairman LRTA

Going to Grenoble has become increasingly fashionable amongst British transport planners and politicians, so much so that there is a danger of dismissing it as overplayed or even overrated. Yet the reality is that while there may be better individual aspects of light rail elsewhere, so far nowhere else comes near it in bringing home the overall impression of the benefits that light rail can bring to a city. Even for those that have been before, there is the new feature of a second route, to the University, opened in November 1990.

100 km south-east of Lyon and 140 km south of Geneva, Grenoble is a city of 160 000 inhabitants (400 000 including adjacent communities), built at the confluence of the Isere and Drac rivers and three mountain valleys, and thus an important regional centre. It is well known for its University (which swells the resident population considerably). Trams ran in the city from 1894 until 1952, when a small trolleybus system was installed to supplement motorbuses on the heaviest corridors.

As with many French private transport operators, the operating company was in a bad way financially by the 1970s, and in 1973 the local authorities decided to assume responsibility for local passenger transport. French Government policy since 1967 has been to encourage groups of adjoining communes (the basic unit of French administration) to join together to form agglomerations for the purpose of producing joint budgets for highways and public transport, and a Syndicat Mixte des Transports en Commun de l'Agglomeration Grenobloise was formed by 24 local authorities to buy a major shareholding in the local and regional bus companies. In 1975 the new mixed shares company SEMITAG was set up to operate local transport, with 64.8% of the capital held by the local authorities, and the remainder by the private company TRANSCET, one of the three French national transport operating consultancies.

The new company set about improving local public transport to counteract the decline in traffic of the previous two decades, provide an alternative for the motorists who were causing congestion in the city centre, and improve the quality of life for the city's inhabitants. The city in its delightful mountain setting has always been environmentally conscious, and the trolleybus system was expanded between 1974 and 1985.

However the narrow streets of the old city centre had difficulty accomodating extra buses, which themselves became caught up in the congestion. The consultancy arm of the Paris RATP was brought in for advice, and recommended a four-route surface tramway system crossing the city centre and serving the main arteries. This coincided with the French Government initiative to encourage the introduction of modern tramways in medium-size cities (including Grenoble). Reasons for recommending trams were the poor productivity of conventional transport, city centre traffic at saturation point, reduced noise and pollution, and possibility to run trams in pedestrian areas in a safe way that could not be achieved with buses. The idea found favour with all the local authorities, with a decision in principle in 1981, followed by various investigations and study trips. After the 1983 elections had provided a stable political base for the future, the matter was put to local referendum, with 53% of those voting declaring in favour of the tramway (the turnout was 37%).This was sufficient to persuade the mayor to give the go ahead.

A programme of public consultation was started, and eventually there were some 450 public meetings in the different districts of the city. A financial plan was drawn up to permit two routes to be built by 1990. The first would link the western suburb of Fontaine with the commercial centre Grand'Place in the south, via the city centre. The second was to link the railway station and the University, sharing city centre tracks with the first line. In February 1984 the French Government agreed to provide FRF 390 million in funding for the project, the balance to be found locally from the versement transport local payroll tax.

This tax is raised on wages through employers of 10 employees or more, and collected through social security contributions. Introduced to Paris in 1971, the ability to raise the tax was extended to provincial cities with over 300 000 inhabitants in 1973, and the population thresholds were lowered to 100 000 in 1974 and 30 000 in 1982. Agglomerations with over 100 000 can charge a basic rate of 1%, but this can be increased up to 1.75% to finance the construction of fixed track transit systems. The Grenoble rate was 1.5%.

One result of the public consultation was the decision to use the introduction of the new tramway to carry out large scale improvements to the urban environment in the central area, through landscaping and extended pedestrianisation, also improving facilities for cyclists along the route of the line. At the same time the motorist was not forgotten, with a large new car park provided near the railway station on the western edge of the city centre, and a new bridge across the Drac, to replace an existing structure which would be confined to trams, pedestrians and cyclists. In coincidence with the reconstruction of the Place de la Gare, a 250 000 m^2 commercial centre was financed by the municipality to attract new businesses.

Construction work started in late 1984, and the first rails were laid in July 1985. The first of the 20 trams ordered from Alsthom was delivered in October 1986. Originally intended to match the so-called French standard tram built for the new system at Nantes, another result of public consultation was the decision to produce a low-floor design, which with 245 mm platforms at each stop would permit almost level access into the car. Two doors were fitted with a small retractable ramp to bridge the gap between platform and car, so that there would be easy access for wheelchairs. Thus disabled people would be able to use a regular public transport service for the first time, and the facilities would also make travelling easier for others. About 60 wheelchair passengers each day now use the tram; a recent survey produced such comments as "the tramway is an extraordinary source of freedom", and "the tramway makes a significant contribution to my integration into city life".

Grenoble tramway line A has been in public service since September 1987. 12 million passengers were carried in the first year, some 26% more than the equivalent bus routes replaced by the tramway. By 1989 18 of the initial fleet of 20 trams were in peak service, with a car every four minutes on the 8.8 km route. Introduction of the tramway permitted 72 buses to be withdrawn from parallel routes; there remain 25 motor and trolleybus routes served by some 200 vehicles, but the trams now carry 30% of the total system patronage, or about 65 000 passengers each day. About 12% of these passengers were not previously public transport users, and 5% of passengers have been identified as former motorists. The overall modal split in the agglomeration had been increased in favour of public transport from 18 to 20%, or about 2000 fewer private car

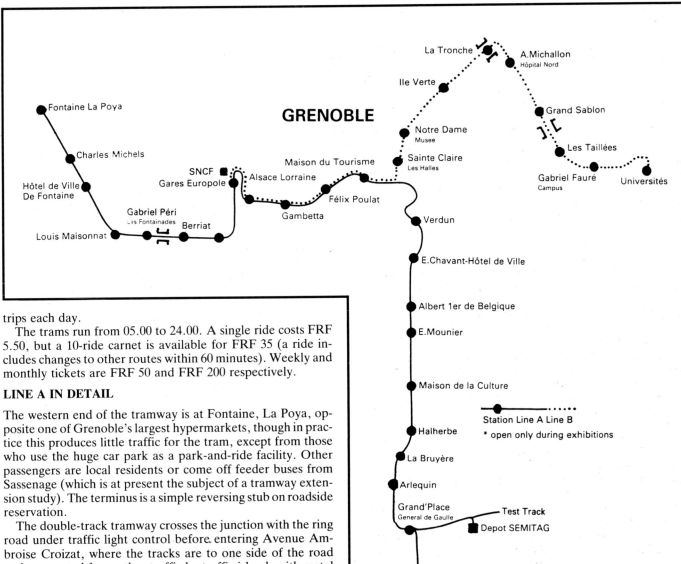

GRENOBLE

Fontaine La Poya

Charles Michels

Hôtel de Ville
De Fontaine

Gabriel Péri
Les Fontainades
Berriat

Louis Maisonnat

SNCF
Gares Europole

Alsace Lorraine

Gambetta

Maison du Tourisme

Félix Poulat

La Tronche

A.Michallon
Hôpital Nord

Ile Verte

Notre Dame
Musee

Sainte Claire
Les Halles

Grand Sablon

Les Taillées

Gabriel Fauré
Campus

Universités

Verdun

E.Chavant-Hôtel de Ville

Albert 1er de Belgique

E.Mounier

Maison de la Culture

Station Line A   Line B

* open only during exhibitions

Halherbe

La Bruyère

Arlequin

Grand'Place
General de Gaulle

Test Track

Depot SEMITAG

Alpexpo*

trips each day.

The trams run from 05.00 to 24.00. A single ride costs FRF 5.50, but a 10-ride carnet is available for FRF 35 (a ride includes changes to other routes within 60 minutes). Weekly and monthly tickets are FRF 50 and FRF 200 respectively.

LINE A IN DETAIL

The western end of the tramway is at Fontaine, La Poya, opposite one of Grenoble's largest hypermarkets, though in practice this produces little traffic for the tram, except from those who use the huge car park as a park-and-ride facility. Other passengers are local residents or come off feeder buses from Sassenage (which is at present the subject of a tramway extension study). The terminus is a simple reversing stub on roadside reservation.

The double-track tramway crosses the junction with the ring road under traffic light control before entering Avenue Ambroise Croizat, where the tracks are to one side of the road and segregated from other traffic by traffic islands with metal fencing. The overhead is strung from bracket arms fixed to every other lamp standard. There are blocks of flats on the north side of the road, but older residences on the south side with the tramway crossing individual accesses and side roads without problem.

The tramway continues into Avenue Aristide Briand, which narrows so that road traffic in one direction moves to an adjacent street just before the important stop Louis Maissonat, where there are shops and restaurants, and bus routes cross to the north and south. The remainder of this street as far as the Drac bridge is given over to the tramway on its full width, with a narrow service lane on some sections. This is possible because through traffic uses a parallel street and the new river bridge. The overhead is supported by wall fixings on buildings.

The Pont du Drac was modified for trams with a new surface above the former road surface, with the void covered by steel plates to give a flush surface. Thus the tramway appears to run on a riased platform, with a cycle track at the old level on the south side and walkways outside the main concrete structure. The bridge crosses the north–south motorway as well as the river.

The tramway is now in Cours Berriat, a busy commercial road wide enough for a tramway reservation on the north side, one lane of motor traffic and kerbside parking (this disappears at tramway stops, where the traffic lane is slewed around the platforms). The reservation has a block finish of different colour to the carriageway, but a low rounded kerb so that motor vehicles can cross it from side roads, or in an emergency. Once again wall fixings mean there are no traction poles.

Approaching the railway bridge, the tramway turns left

The terminus of the line at Fontaine La Poya is a simple stub, quite adequate for reversing a 4 minute service of double-ended cars.

M.R. Taplin

▲ The remodelled Pont du Drac with the cycleway at the original level on the right hand side and the tramway on its new platform.
Peter Fox

◀ Cours Berriat stop with the protected stop and residual carriageway use for road traffic.
M.R. Taplin

▼ A short subway takes the tramway under the SNCF rail tracks to link Cours Berriat with the railway station.
M.R. Taplin

▲▲ Gares Europoles is the name for the stop serving the rail and bus stations, with direct access to the TGV platform of the former. The central track is used for reversing cars on route B from December 1990.
Peter Fox

▲ Rue Felix Poulat is the commercial centre of Grenoble and was once a melee of cars and buses with pedestrians confined to narrow pavements. Now the trams and pedestrians co-exist safely together. *M.R. Taplin*

▶ The sharp curve in the narrow street from rue Raoul Blanchard to Place de Verdun, where the building on the left was colonnaded to provide pedestrian facilities. Other traffic can make a right turn under guidance of a warning signal. *M.R. Taplin*

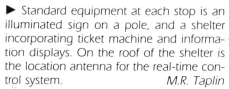

◀ A Grenoble tram leans to the curve as it articulates gracefully around Place de Verdun on a low reservation.   *M.R. Taplin*

▶ Standard equipment at each stop is an illuminated sign on a pole, and a shelter incorporating ticket machine and information displays. On the roof of the shelter is the location antenna for the real-time control system.   *M.R. Taplin*

◀ In the newer suburbs the tramway is an effective instrument of traffic calming, with restricted access to garages for residents.   *M.R. Taplin*

▶ The junction for route B under construction in August 1990. The alignment of this line through Place Ste Claire was varied from the original plans when Roman remains were discovered during excavation for services.   *M.R. Taplin*

under traffic signal control and dives under the railway in a steeply-graded private underpass from where the tracks rise gently to the station stop adjacent to the SNCF platforms. This stop has a reversing siding for route B. A 180 degree turn around the ticket office and station gardens shows how quietly the vehicles can traverse a 25 m curve. Wiring is suspended from some modern art lighting pillars; a judgement on their aesthetics would be a matter of personal taste.

Passing lawns and fountains the tramway swings into Avenue Alsace-Lorraine, nominally a tram and pedestrian street, but with limited time-restricted access for deliveries from side roads. Tree planting has produced a green and shady environment, just right for the pavement cafes, for this is one of the main commercial streets leading to the city centre. At the crossing with Cours Jean Jaures the overhead is suspended from a monumental metal sculpture, built as a work of art at the same time as the tramway.

Beside Place Victor Hugo the tramway is separated from a lane of motor traffic by massive white stones every metre as it swings into the pedestrianised Rue Felix Poulat. This street is more like a square and is the effective city centre, with a

bustle of pedestrians who show little awareness of the trams gliding through their mist. Just a few years ago this was a melee of buses, cars, noise and fumes, with pedestrians confined to the pavements. Now it is a civilised place to work, shop or stroll. The tram tracks curve across the square and round a sharp bend into the still pedestrianised Rue Raoul Blanchard.

After a stop adjacent to the Tourist Office the tramway is back in a limited access street, and here is located the junction for line B to the University. Immediately there is one of the most interesting sections of the line, as the street narrows almost to the width of the tramway, with old buildings each side and a sharp bend past the Stendahl School. Here there was no room for pedestrians, so the municipality bought the ground-floor frontages of the buildings and created a pedestrian arcade. The effect is most attractive.

The tramway now runs around the edge of the tree-lined Pl de Verdun, crossing traffic lanes with priority that does not seem to need enforcement by traffic signals. One road leading south from the Square is reserved for the tramway, pedestrians and narrow service access for frontagers, and here again there are pavement cafes between tramway and shop fronts,

with relaxed patrons enjoying their aperitifs.

Curving round into Place Pasteur, buses are permitted to share the tramway reservation in one direction to give them priority through a busy junction with the main east–west traffic artery across the city. This is controlled by traffic lights, and here some traction poles are necessary beacuse adjacent build-

ings are too far away for the overhead to be strung from wall fixings. The tramway is now alongside the long straight highway to the southern suburbs, Avenue Marcelin Berthelot. Most of this has been converted to one-way for motor traffic, which occupies two lanes, then comes the tramway reservation, cycle path and pavement for pedestrians. Northbound road traffic uses Avenue Perrot, a block or so to the east.

The tramway enters the modern part of Grenoble, and leaves the main highway to run past tall blocks of flats along streets where traffic calming measures mean only the locals know how to gain access, and the tramway and cycle path can be fitted in with the residual traffic. A section of tree-lined private right of way cuts a corner into Rue Dodero, where through traffic (apart from cyclists) is prevented by the tram stop occupying the full width of the road. Each stop is to a standard design, with an attractive shelter containing map, timetable information, ticket machine and litter bin.

Soon the tramway swings into Grand'Place General de Gaulle, where the interchange station is the most impressive structure on the system. Here three bus routes terminate and three others pass by. The station is a modern overall-roofed structure with the tram tracks in the centre and buses at the edge, to give cross-platform interchange. There are kiosks and a ticket office, while a footbridge gives access to the adjacent commercial centre including shops, restaurants, offices and the Hotel Mercure. This is the regular tramway terminus, and trams turn around the large roundabout immediately beyond, but south of this roundabout there is 600 m of track to the Alpexpo exhibition centre, which sees special services whenever an event in scheduled there.

East of the roundabout a 1 km central reservation accomodates two tram tracks leading to Eybens tram depot, where the control centre for the system is located. Here there are 12 storage tracks, and a four-track maintenance area equipped with high-level walkways to give easy access to the roof-mounted electrical equipment. There is also a paint shop, body shop, jacking gear for lifting bodies from their bogies, a wheel lathe and a car washer. A fenced test track permits trials at full line speed. The control centre can monitor the position of every tram in service by radio and an automatic recorder on the roof of the shelter at every tram stop.There are five re-motely-controlled sub stations. Overhead wire is 120 mm^2 copper supported by ICI Parafil synthetic span wires every 60 m. Track is grooved rail weighing 55.29 kg/m.

The direct cost of tram route A (including rolling stock) was FRF 585 million; in addition FRF 154 million went on other public transport improvements associated with the introduction of the tramway, FRF 146 million was spent on works benefitting traffic in general and FRF 300 million on environmental projects along the line of route. The people of Grenoble are delighted with the results.

LINE B

Since 24th November 1990, a second line, line B has been open. This 4.6 km extension with nine new stops runs from the junction with line A, north and east via Avenue Marechal Randon to the hospital, university halls of residence and the University itself. It crosses the River Isere twice, once on a 28 m bridge shared with road traffic and once on a 465 m viaduct reserved for trams, cyclists and pedestrians. A through service is operated as line B from the University to the railway station, sharing tracks with line A through the city centre. Two bus routes were replaced and others rerouted in a feeder role.

The inauguration on 24th November marked the start of a four-day festival of illuminations and events that focussed the attention of the whole city on its new public transport facility. The large contingent from British local authorities who were invited to attend came away envious of what has been achieved, and anxious to bring similar benefits to their own cities.

◀ The terminus at Grand'Place–General de Gaulle is an impressive structure forming an interchange and with access to the adjacent commercial centres which are still under development. The trams turn on the inside of a traffic roundabout. *M.R. Taplin*

▼ 280 mm high platform to 345 mm high car floor provides easy access for all, while for wheelchairs the two centre doors feature sliding ramps.
M.R. Taplin

◀▼ Some of the Roman remains referred to on the previous page.
Peter Fox

Transcorp is a consortium of three companies specialising in transportation systems, bringing together Architecture, Engineering, Ergonomics, Rolling Stock Design, Industrial, Environmental, Retail, Corporate and Graphic Design.

Transcorp brings a new approach to the challenges and demands of Light Rail Systems for the future.

Each city has its unique character, so do its people, so do its transport solutions. Transcorp has the ability to assist you in realising your project objectives.

Our collective international experience will address the problems associated with the design and development of these important transport initiatives. From feasibility through to rolling stock and architectural infrastructure, our philosophy is simple: **it is people who are important.**

Transcorp

For further information, please contact Peter Trickett on 071·434 0887/0517 Fax: 071·434 0269

HANNOVER
25 Years of Light Rail Development
by Dr. Richard J. Buckley

THE CITY

The city of Hannover dates from the mid-twelfth century. It has a long history as a commercial centre and was at one time a member of the Hanseatic League. Nineteenth century developments gave it an important manufacturing base too and the city is today the site of the largest industrial exhibition in the world, the annual April Fair. Between 1714 and 1837 Britain and Hannover shared a royal house, an era recalled by the delightful summer palace gardens at Herrenhausen; a small museum there houses some sculptures by the noted Sheffield artist, Sir Francis Chantrey. Hannover still has a governmental role as the capital of Lower Saxony. The city is today almost entirely modern and has a population of 514 000, with up to twice as many using it as a shopping and employment centre.

THE DEVELOPMENT OF PUBLIC TRANSPORT

Local public transport followed the usual late-nineteenth century pattern, developing from horse buses (1852) through horse trams (1872) to electric trams (1893). The latter had several points of interest, particularly the early construction of several long rural lines and a high-speed interurban to the neighbouring town of Hildesheim. Freight traffic was a very important source of revenue on these out-of-town tramways. By 1906 the system had a route length of 162.2 km, which made it the most extensive in Germany outside Berlin. From 1921 the operating company became known as the *Überlandwerke und Strassenbahn AG* as an indication of its additional interests in electricity generation and supply; despite subsequent changes in title, ownership and sphere of operation, the undertaking is still universally known by the acronym ÜSTRA.

As well as trams, motorbuses have been operated since 1925 and launches (on the Machsee) since 1936; between 1937 and 1958 there was a trolleybus route as well. Despite this, and even though the tramway network was almost completely reconstructed after World War II, the rail system survived almost unaltered until the 1950s. Fleet and infrastructure modernisation was ongoing, of course; the percentage of reserved to street track rose from 12% to 39% between 1937 and 1970, for instance, and in the early 1950s ÜSTRA was closely involved in the development and introduction of the bogie *Grossraumwagen* (high-capacity tram). At this time it was decided to close most of the rural tramways, because after the loss of freight to road transport passenger traffic alone did not justify a tramway service. By 1960/61 both fleet modernisation and route contraction had been largely achieved; all pre-war wooden bodied trams had been withdrawn and all except one half of the one out-of-town route had been closed. In partial compensation, four urban lines were extended between 1947 and 1965, and by the latter date a few six-axle articulated trams with bogie trailers had been added to the fleet to complete its post-war renewal (although pre and post-war two-axle cars were still required for peak hour services until 1977).

STADTBAHN: PLANNING

Stadtbahn means simply an urban railway. In German usage this can mean anything from a suburban railway operated by and on the principles of a main-line railway (as in Berlin), through fully-segregated light rail (as in the Ruhr) to light rail combining fully, partially and non-segregated sections; each may or may not include underground sections, which are then somewhat confusingly described as *U-Bahnen* (underground railways). The Hannover Stadtbahn does include an extensive underground network, but otherwise is at the lighter end of the definition. Its history to date, whilst not unique, illustrates very clearly how a light rail system can be successfully developed by incremental stages from an existing street tramway network and can partake the advantages of both modes.

The necessity of replacing the tramways by light rail might

A number of the 500 series six-axle cars are still in use on the remaining street routes. This photograph shows No. 508 repainted in pop-art livery with trailer 1504 in the more conventional green livery on Route 18 Nordhafen–Rathaus outside the Hauptbahnhof on 12th September 1990.   *Peter Fox*

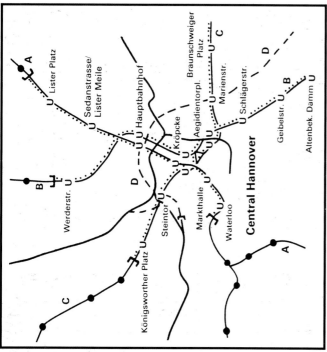

Central Hannover

▲ The entrance to the main city centre interchange station, Kröpcke, is from a below-ground-level pedestrian mall known as *die Passerelle.* The area above this is also pedestrianised. *Peter Fox*

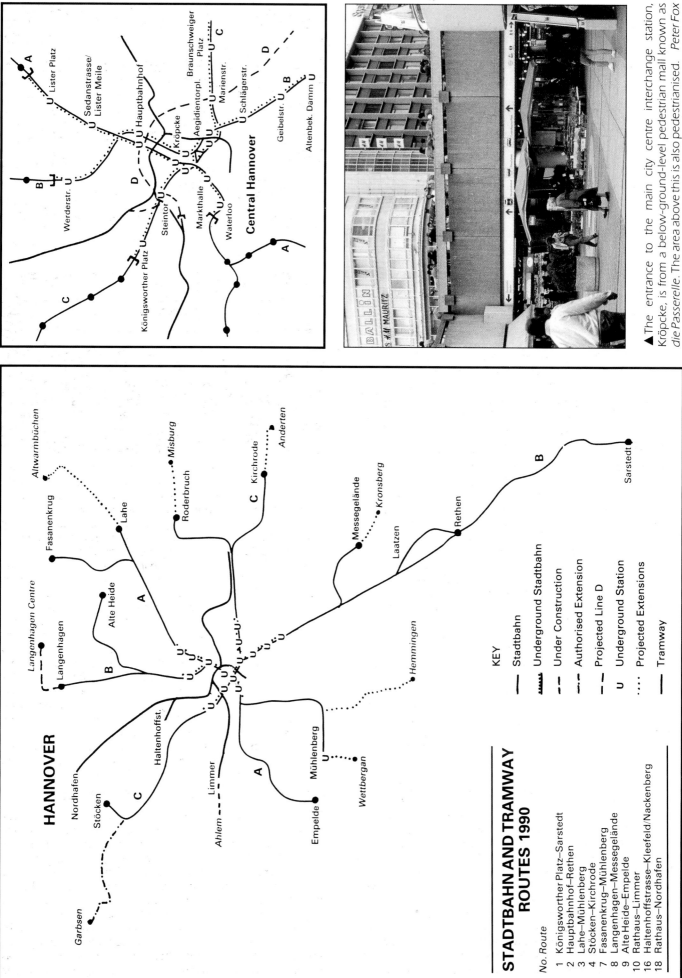

HANNOVER

STADTBAHN AND TRAMWAY ROUTES 1990

No. Route
1 Königsworther Platz–Sarstedt
2 Hauptbahnhof–Rethen
3 Lahe–Mühlenberg
4 Stöcken–Kirchrode
7 Fasanenkrug–Mühlenberg
8 Langenhagen–Messegelände
9 Alte Heide–Empelde
10 Rathaus–Limmer
16 Haltenhoffstrasse–Kleefeld/Nackenberg
18 Rathaus–Nordhafen

KEY
— Stadtbahn
╌╌╌ Underground Stadtbahn
–·–· Under Construction
– – – Authorised Extension
U Projected Line D
∪ Underground Station
········ Projected Extensions
— Tramway

▲The tramway station outside Hannover Hauptbahnhof. This may be replaced at some time in the future by the D-tunnel.
Peter Fox

▼Platform level at Kröpcke with a Route 1 two-car train bound for Königsworther Platz. *Peter Fox*

▲▼These two view of the interior of the Kröpcke interchange give some idea of its size. *Peter Fox*

seem obvious today, but in the early 1960s Hannover, with a modern tramway and integrated bus service, already had an excellent transport system; how, then, was the cost and inconvenience of Stadtbahn construction justified at that time?

The underlying rationale was the need to adjust to changes foreseen in the city and its economic region during the ensuing decades. So far as these affected transport, they were broadly summarised under three headings– traffic, population and quality of life. First, the post-war traffic plan drawn up in 1949 envisaged that car ownership would rise from the then rate of 1:69 citizens to 1:10 and road schemes – such as the construction of an inner ring road – were laid accordingly. Yet already by 1960 this supposed maximum had been reached and by 1965 the ratio had become 1:5. In 1962 it was estimated that allowing motor traffic to increase unchecked would require parking spaces to be multiplied ten times over which would take up an area greater than the entire inner city (assuming all parking was at street level). Motorisation on this scale, it was realised, would cause severe traffic congestion in the short term and unnaccceptable destruction of the city for road building in the long term; subsequent experience the world over has shown that even massive investment in roads does not remove traffic congestion in any case.

Population changes were also important. In the 1960s people were being moved out of congested inner areas to new estates on the outskirts of the city. There were also the first signs of the trend towards suburban homes in former village communities outside Hannover proper, whose population has actually been steadily falling from a peak of 575 000 in 1960 to today's 514 000. Since over 75% of the region's jobs remained in Hannover, an increasing proportion of those in the city centre, more and longer journeys to work would result.

The quality of life argument seems to have gained in importance as the scheme proceeded. In the early days it was only said that streets freed from heavy traffic could be better used by the remaining cars and pedestrians. Since then, as enviromental concerns have risen to the top of the agenda, the Stadtbahn has been described as bringing life back to the city,

as, for instance, by the associated construction of a new walkway from Kröpcke to the Hauptbahnhof. It has also made possible various other pedestrianisation schemes, such as along much of the main shopping street, Georgstrasse.

If the increasing number of people wishing to reach the city centre could not be accommodated on the roads, then public transport would have to take a greater share. By 1979 the ratio between public and private transport within the city was 38:62; for commuters it was 45:55 and for commuters travelling from outside the city it was 65:35. The aim was to improve these latter proportions to 55:45 and 70:30. But this would only be possible if public transport were radically improved to make it more attractive to commuters, including the increasing proportion of car owners. The speed of public transport needed to be maintained or even increased to take acount of longer journeys. In the face of traffic congestion it was thought that this could only be achieved by putting public transport on a 'second level', in German terms usually in tunnel but occasionally on a viaduct. Easy transfer with buses or – via Park and Ride schemes – with cars was also important. At the same time it was desired to retain the dense network and easy access and transfer typical of tramways. The Stadtbahn was seen as the mode best suited to meet these conflicting objectives.

STADTBAHN: CONSTRUCTION AND OPERATION

The original Stadtbahn plans drawn up in the early 1960s envisaged four cross-city underground lines designed to include most existing surface tramway services. These were lines A (blue), B (red), C (yellow) and D (green). The underground stations were to have high platforms whereas, in general, the surface lines were to retain pavement-level access. In this respect the Hannover plans differed from those in, say, Köln in that traditional tramcars could not be used (unless specially adapted, as a few were, but never actually used underground). The four-line plan has been broadly adhered to throughout, though improvements have been incorporated as time has progressed and some details have been changed. One change to the planned network was the decision to retain all the re mainder whole of the former interurban line instead of cutting it back to Heisede, a few kilometres short of Sarstedt. There has also been some vacillation over the tram routes to Nordhafen and Haltenhoffstrasse, which earlier plans sometimes omitted from the Stadtbahn system; however work is now in progress to link them into line C.

The first pile for the Stadtbahn was driven on 16th November 1966 at Waterlooplatz, on the future line A. Most tunnels have been constructed on the invasive but relatively cheap cut-and-cover method, but a few tubes have had to be driven underneath buildings, for instance between Aegidientorplatz (usually abbreviated to 'Aegi') and Marienstrasse on line C-Ost. The system has developed from 1965 to date as shown in Table I.

As each tunnel section was brought into use, connecting surface lines were upgraded to Stadtbahn standard. Wherever practicable, this means using existing or new reserved tracks. But it has rarely been possible to fully upgrade any line by the opening date and line C–West to Stöcken was the first time that this was done. More usually, piecemeal improvements have still had to be carried out later. For example, work has only recently been completed on a new central reservation along part of Hildesheimer Strasse, although the B-Süd tunnel has been open since 1982. Even then, some sections will retain

street running for the foreseeable future. The Kirchrode branch of line C-West has street tracks, for instance, because of the existing building line and the trees alongside the Tiergarten.

Whether reserved or not, surface lines are still crossed by other traffic at intersections. Over much of the system Stadtbahn cars have no means of influencing the traffic lights, and this can produce marked delays. However ÜSTRA has developed a technology (the BON system) to allow priority for LRVs and the line from Döhrener Turm to Bothmerstrasse (B-Süd) was adapted to it in 1989. In time it will be extended to the whole network, at a cost of DM 20 million, with consequent improvements in punctuality and speed. It is, of course, essential for cars to arrive at the tunnel ramps as promptly as possible so that tunnel capacity is not reduced by delays. The train control system can deal with up to thirty trains per hour per direction underground. When three car trains are used (except for off-peak services, two car trains are the norm) for the annual trade fair, 13 000 passengers can be moved per hour per direction.

A further improvement to surface lines is the provision of high platforms (matching those at underground stations), especially at places where cross-platform interchange is provided with feeder buses, such as at the newly-built Lahe terminus

TABLE I. STADTBAHN OPENING DATES

Date	Tunnel	New Surface Line
30/09/73		Urfeldstrasse–Laatzen Sud (B)
26/10/75	Hbf–Waterloo (A)	
04/04/76	Hbf–Lister Platz (A)	Buchholz–Lahe (A)
18/06/76		Laatzen Sud–Rethen (B)
25/09/77	Oberricklingen–Mühlenburg (A)	
01/10/78		Nackenberg–Medizinische Hochschule (C)
27/05/79	Kröpcke–Vahrenwalder Platz (B)	Vahrenheide–Alte Heide (B)
30/05/81	Hbf–Schlägerstrasse (B)	
26/09/82	Schlägerstrasse–Döhrener Turm	
30/03/84	Kröpcke–Steintor (C)	
29/09/84		Medizinische Hochschule–Roderbruch* (C)
26/06/85	Steintor–Königsworther Platz (C)	
24/04/88		Langenhagen extension (B)
24/09/89	Aegi–Braunschweig Platz (C)	

* Includes a short tunnel

ÜSTRA

▼Two Duewag Stadtbahn cars at Wallensteinstrasse, a short-working point on the original stadtbahn line A, photographed in May 1977.   *R.J. Buckley*

▲The surface buildings at Aegidientorplatz underground station incorporate a snackbar and a ticket machine. *Peter Fox*

▲▶A two-car stadtbahn train at Rethen Nord on the interurban line to Sarstedt; this is a typical low-platform station. *R.J. Buckley*

▶Sarstedt terminus has a low platform and convenient bus interchange. *Peter Fox*

▼The terminus a Lahe has high platforms with the road at higher level allowing cross platform interchange with connecting buses. *R.J. Buckley*

or the rebuilt one at Stöcken. But intermediate stops are also being rebuilt, most recently at Laatzen Nord and Eichstrasse (on line B-Süd), the first time high platforms have been placed in the centre of the carriageway rather than at the side or off-street. There are definite plans to improve seventeen other stops and up to sixty five more may be included later if financial and planning constraints can be overcome. With those completed already, this would leave only a few low-platform stops on the existing system, but such a stage would not be reached for many years.

ÜSTRA runs an integrated network of light rail vehicles and buses, and both also run in conjunction with main-line rail and other bus services too. The organisation and tariff structure (basically a three-zone two-price fare) is provided by the *Grossraum-Verkehr Hannover*, established in 1970. There are bus–Stadtbahn interchanges at various points on the system, including most termini, and, at places such as Lahe, large car parks as well.

The Stadtbahn network and tram Route 10 are served by a current fleet of 230 eight-axle double-ended cars, with a further twenty on order. The two other tram services are operated by elderly six-axle articulated trams towing bogie trailers; the new Stadtbahn cars will replace these in 1991–92. The latter were designed in conjunction with Duewag in the early 1970s and subsequent deliveries – built from 1979 under licence by Linke-Hoffman-Busch – have retained the original design almost unaltered. The only significant change has been the fitting of more modern AEG thyristor control equipment from 1988 deliveries onwards. The most distinctive operating feature of these cars is the retractable step which enables them to serve both high and low (pavement level) platforms with equal ease. This has been a key element in the gradual and flexible development of a Stadtbahn from the former street tramway. The now standard ÜSTRA lime-green livery was inaugurated by these cars as well, all part of the important task of giving the new mode a new image.

To service the Stadtbahn fleet, existing depots at Buchholz, Glocksee and Vahrenheide have been used and adapted where necessary. A completely new depot has replaced the old one at Döhren. Glocksee works has been rebuilt in stages since 1986; over half has been completed and by 1995 there will be eighteen tracks available to maintain the present cars. The works will also be able to deal with any future new types of vehicle.

By the time the C-Ost subway along Marienstrasse was opened in autumn 1989, the Stadtbahn system had reached a route length of 80 km out of a total network of 97 km. Back in 1967 the tramways shared 65% of their route with other traffic on street. Today 15% is in tunnel, 60% on reserved track and only 25% in the street. There are 125 Stadtbahn stops, sixteen of which are underground stations, and eight Stadtbahn routes running over the three basic lines so far built. 143 km of new track has been laid, 29 km of this in tunnel.

The present route network is shown on the map. The routes with double digits are tram services. On the Stadtbahn services the blue, red and yellow 'line' colours are used to indicate directions etc at underground stations. Where a route uses two tunnels, both colours are used. This scheme has its merits, but is not altogether closely related to the current route map, which allcates each service a seperate colour. This is normally a shade of blue for line A, red for line B etc., but the scheme breaks down when it comes to 'cross-tunnel' services. Tunnel colours make sense where lines operate independently, as on the London Underground, but they are less successful on a unified network.

Over two thousand million DM has been invested in the Stadtbahn to date. Most of the capital cost for the infrastructure is funded as follows – 60% from the Federal Government, 25% from Lower Saxony and 15% from the City and from ÜSTRA itself. A small proportion for items such as planning, design and administration is left for ÜSTRA to meet from its own resources. The new cars and a proportion of surface track and depot reconstruction have to be paid for by ÜSTRA, though of course this is also publicly funded by either the City or the Grossaum Verkehr, each of which have shares in ÜSTRA's holding company. Exceptionally, Lower Saxony is paying half the cost of the twenty new cars on order.

TABLE II.
TECHNICAL DATA FOR STADTBAHN CARS

Fleet numbers	6001–6230 (6231–50 on order)
Building dates	1974–1989 (in four series)
Axle arrangement	B'2'2'B
Motor rating (kW)	2 x 217
Maximum speed (km/h)	80
Length overall (m)	28.28
Width overall (m)	2.4
Body height (m)	3.31
Floor height (mm)	943
Step heights (mm)	388/294/261 (when using low platform)
Weight unladen (kg)	38.8
Seats	46 (6176–90 have 52)
Standing (4 m²)	104
Minimum curve radius (m)	17.5
Maximum acceleration (m/s²)	1.0
Emergency braking (m/s²)	3.0

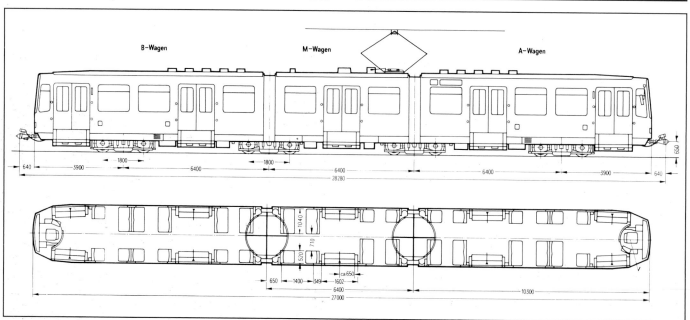

STADTBAHN: RESULTS

Such a large expenditure must naturally lead to one to question, has the aim of Stadtbahn construction been achieved? This was to seperate public from private transport as far as possible and thereby to obtain a more regular, punctual, fast and comfortable service able to compete on level terms with private cars.

The quality of service has certainly been improved. In terms of speed, the old tram route from Fasanenkrug to Oberricklingen (the terminus before the extension to Mühlenberg was built) took 48 minutes to complete the journey; the Stadtbahn reduced this to 40 minutes and raised the service speed from 19.6 km/h to 24 km/h. Of even more importance to passengers is regularity and punctuality. Again on Route 7, peak hour delays to trams of 20 minutes were not uncommon, which meant long waits at stops and overcrowded vehicles. Whereas Stadtbahn delays are minimal and do not produce overcrowding, the increased capacity of Stadtbahn cars and their ability to run through without obstruction also results in a more comfortable journey. A particularly significant feature of the Hannover Stadtbahn has been the manner in which the convenience and acessibility of the trams has been retained. Virtually no tramway stops have been lost, even when replaced by underground stations (although stop distances were traditionally much greater than in Britain anyway). Nowhere in the inner city is more than five minutes from an underground station. And interchange is planned to take no longer than changing trams (though at the multi-level Kröpcke station one has to question whether this has been achieved).

Given that public transport has been improved by the Stadtbahn, have the desired results followed?

So far as motorisation is concerned, it is a fact that whereas almost 475 per 1000 inhabitants of the (former) Federal Republic had a motor car in 1988, less than 375 per 1000 did in Hannover. There could be all sorts of reasons for this, such differences in income or a lower propensity to drive in a city as opposed to rural areas, but the existence of good public transport cannot be without influence. When it comes to the modal split between public and private transport, the only available figure is for all passengers within the city, which is currently 40:60. This is marginally better than the 1979 ratio of 38:62, but not a great deal better. It is questionable, therefore, whether the targets mentioned earlier for commuters have been achieved. However, the Stadtbahn undoubtedly has increased its traffic as against tramway operation. The initial routes using line A recorded rises of approximately 50%. Much of this was transfer traffic from newly integrated bus services etc., but 15–20% of the increase was found to be new traffic to public transport. Overall, ÜSTRA has shown a 15% rise in traffic since the first Stadtbahn line was opened in 1975, while at 0.7 trips per inhabitant per day Hannover has one of the highest usage rates for public transport for comparable cities in West Germany.

Environmentally, the Stadtbahn has certainly made possible a radical restructuring of the city centre, with extensive connected pedestrian zones and a free passage underneath the Hauptbahnhof. This latter area, *die Passerelle*, is in fact rather unpleasant at times, with a quantity of litter from fast food outlets and with undesireables drinking alcohol around the stairways. Though of course it would be unfair to blame the transport mode for the use people make of the facilities provided.

With regard to other environmental benefits, it is naturally the case that where trams have gone underground – and still more so where streets have been pedestrianised – the noise levels are much reduced. In Lister Meile, for example, the maximum was about 79 dBA in 1965, whereas in 1985 it was only 69 dBA. Every car passenger attracted to the Stadtbahn means a reduction in atmospheric pollution too, as per Table III.

One obvious fault in the early planning was that no account was taken of disabled people. From street level passengers have to climb three steps to board the Stadtbahn cars. And at the original underground stations entry and exit was always by escalators and stairs. In 1984 when Steintor station was opened there was a protest by wheelchair users at lack of access to the Stadtbahn. More recent construction has borne this in mind and on line C-Ost the underground stations have lifts and high-platform surface stops have ramps. This will, however, be of only limited value until the central area stations have wheelchair access too. This question has, it is true, only recently risen to the top of the agenda and it is perhaps unfair to expect planners in the 1960s to have foreseen it.

Commercially, the Stadtbahn has proved more economic to operate than the trams. Comparisons made in 1976 between Stadtbahn line A and former tram services showed that although the Stadtbahn cost more to run, its higher earnings reduced the operating deficit by about 20%. On the expenditure side, the high-capacity cars require fewer drivers, so wage costs are reduced. Energy efficient technology also allows the return of up to 25% of the current used to the overhead.

In 1975 ÜSTRA's cost recovery was 59.5%, whereas by the early 1980s it had become 70%. Since then it has fallen again to 65.7%, but this is still markedly better than the average for all West German public transport undertakings, which is only 53% (1988 figures). The rising deficit is causing concern and various possible ways of dealing with it have been canvassed. In the worst-case scenario, by the year 2000 bus services would be cut or even entirely abandoned and rail services would be withdrawn in the evenings and all day on Sundays. The consequence, of course, would be a huge increase in motor traffic and the need for thousands more parking places in the city, just the things the Stadtbahn has been designed to avoid. The alternative 'offensive scenario' would involve positive marketing to attract more passengers which, if successful, would actually produce the smallest rise in the deficit and thus be of the greatest all-round benefit.

STADTBAHN: FUTURE PROSPECTS

Currently ÜSTRA operates eight Stadtbahn routes over the completed sections of lines A, B and C. There are still three surface tramway routes, Route 10 to Limmer, Route 18 to Nordhafen and Route 16, which runs across the city from Nackenburg via Zoo to Haltenhoffstrasse. The Nordhafen/Haltenhoffstrasse branch will be brought into a new C-Nord tunnel, which is now being built, in 1993. This will have two stations, at Christuskirche and Kopernikusstrasse, before surfacing just beyond Lutherkirche.

This will leave trams running to Limmer and to Zoo/Stadt-

▼Surface tracks in the middle of the road are gradually being converted from tramway type to ballasted railway-type. This photograph shows a temporary single-line station where engineering work is under way.   *Peter Fox*

◄New high-platform stations in the middle of the road are being built on the Sarstedt route. This photograph taken at Laatzen Nord shows one such station. Functionally they are good, but they do nothing to enhance the environment.   *Peter Fox*

halle. It has always been intended that the Limmer route should be covered by Stadtbahn line D (green). This was projected through the city via Steintor, Hauptbahnhof and Marienstrasse to an underground terminus at Waldheim, in an area not previously served by tram. Line D, as planned, would pass under the existing subways and some basic work on its stations was therefore carried out when the first tunnels were built. Surprisingly, therefore, there is currently some discussion about whether line D should run under or overground in the city. ÜSTRA, or at least some people within it, seem now to favour the surface option, whereas the city authorities are pressing for all routes to be underground. A surface line could connect with Route 16 to Zoo/Stadthalle, possibly with the aid of pedestrianised or traffic-calmed streets, and sketches of this option exist. This contradicts most earlier plans, which envisaged the closure of this tramway, with Zoo/ Stadthalle being served only by Stadtbahn cars running along Marienstrasse. A further variable has been thrown into the debate by the decision to hold the world exhibition Expo 2000 in Hannover. A public transport link to the site at Kronsberg beyond Messgelände will be essential. An S-Bahn rail link is a possibility, but post-Expo travel expectations make a Stadtbahn service more likely. There are two possibilities, either an extension of Route 8 under the Messe site or the construction of Line D further than originally envisaged, to Kronsberg. If built, this would be worked by new 2.65 m wide stock.

When the original plans were made for the Stadtbahn, the cases for a 'second level' seems to have been accepted more-or-less without debate. The debate over line D has already been referred to. In addition to this, ÜSTRA have long-term plans for another surface operation in the inner city, an environmentally friendly City-Bus route, probably using minibuses powered by some kind of alternative technology. So there is some evidence of second thoughts about the underground option. However, it is difficult to envisage that surface light rail would have proved adequate to Hannover's needs. Firstly, motor traffic still requires access to the city centre, particularly to the station area, which was – and to some extent still is – one of the main tramway arteries. Conflicting traffic movements here and in other central locations would have been bound to hold up rail services to an unacceptable extent. Secondly, through motor traffic has been diverted onto a multi-lane inner ring road encircling the centre at a distance of about 1 km. All the radial public transport services must cross this and clearly cannot effectively do so on the level. Thirdly, because of the extended journeys consequent on population movements, fast trips are important. Relatively slow services through traffic malls cannot provide the same quick access to and through the city centre as can underground railways.

The plans for suburban extensions beyond the present ter-

mini are clearer than those for line D. Work is in progress to take line B-Nord into the centre of Langenhagen; this should be completed by 1991 together with a new bus interchange. Funds are also secured to extend line C-West from Stöcken to Garbsen and line D-West from Limmer to Ahlem; these three total 10 km of new route. Medium term prospects are for extension of A-Süd from Mühlenburg to Wettbergen and of C-Ost from Kirchrode to Anderten. In discussion are lines from Lahe to Altwarmbüchen, Ricklingen to Hemmingen, Roderbruch to Misburg and Messegelände to Kronsberg. Many of these would include new bus interchanges and park-and-ride car parks.

Apart from expanding the system in this way, ÜSTRA has another long term aim by which to improve the service. This is to increase the seating capacity on the Stadtbahn, which currently is only 46 per car as opposed to 104 standing. This has always been quite a normal proportion on European light railways, but it is evidently felt that car-owning commuters will increasingly want to be seated. The preferred option is to run 2.65 m wide cars instead of the present 2.40 m wide stock, which would allow a 60% increase in seats within the same length. Most tracks could already permit such cars, but the rest of the surface network would have to be adapted to match. Since the existing modern fleet is virtually complete, no new cars could be in service before the year 2000. There is, incidentally, no longer any talk of turning the system into a full U-Bahn, which had at one time been mooted.

ÜSTRA has developed some advanced technologies for the Stadtbahn in conjunction with government and commercial partners. These are marketed to other operators through a consultancy subsidiary, TransTec. It has not been possible to cover this matter here, but hopefully enough has been said to show that Hannover is one of the world leaders in light rail. The Stadtbahn, as it is continuously adapted, improved and extended, will provide the city and its economic region with efficient, economic and attractive public transport well into the next century.

ACKNOWLEDGEMENTS

I am very grateful to ÜSTRA Hannoversche Verkehrsbetriebe AG for the supply of various items published by themselves, by the Landeshauptstadt Hannover (U-Bahn-Bauamt) and by the Grossraum-Verkehr Hannover (GVH). Amongst the most useful have been the following:
GVH 20 Jahre Grossraum-Verkehr Hannover (1990)
ÜSTRA Linien (2/1979)
ÜSTRA Nahverkehr in Hannover: das Konzept der ÜSTRA (1989)
Stadt Stadtbahn Hannover: Linie C-Ost (1989)
ÜSTRA Stadtbahn-System Hannover (1989)
Any opinions expressed are, of course, my own.

CITY OF THE AUTOMOBILE
Los Angeles looks to Light Rail
by Michael Taplin

Before his first visit to Los Angeles the writer can always remember being solemnly told by a travel agent that it would be absolutely necessary to hire a car there, since there was no public transport in the Californian city. Fortunately I knew better than the travel agent, but the myth that this sprawling metropolis is given over entirely to the private car has some grains of truth. Certainly the post-war planners at one time believed that it was possible to meet everyone's desire for personal transport, and made a sustained effort to build the infrastructure necessary to support this lifestyle.

A little history is necessary to put this in perspective. Founded by the Spanish colonialists in 1781, when Los Angeles became part of the 31st state of the USA in 1850 it boasted a population of just 2200. This had trebled by 1873 when the first horse tramway franchises were granted. The railways came in 1876 (Southern Pacific) and 1885 (Santa Fe), and a crude electric line was demonstrated in 1887. By the turn of the century 102 500 populated the expanding city limits.

The next two decades saw the establishment and consolidation of what many regard as the finest passenger transportation system of the time, Henry E. Huntington's fabled Pacific Electric, which demonstrated the vital link between efficient public transport and real estate development, with an interurban network that supported the growth of the city to two million inhabitants, and the metropolitan area to over four million. The Los Angeles Railway ran a network of 3'6" gauge city tramways. However although Los Angeles was America's largest city in area (1560 square miles) it had a very low density of

population, around 4400 per square mile (compared with 25 000 in New York, and 16 000 in Boston and Chicago). Thus the passenger rail networks were easy targets for motorisation, and abandonment started in the 1930s.

To cope with the growth in population and motor traffic, an ambitious freeway (grade separated motorway) and expressway (limited-access highway) programme was started with the aim of having 1280 miles of such roads built by 1980. However even before the last of the Pacific Electric's Big Red Cars ran in 1961 (and the last city tramway in 1963), someone had identified that in what passes for the city centre, 28% of the land was taken up by highways and a further 38% by off-street parking/loading facilities, and the pedestrian was regarded as something of an anachronism in the suburbs. Even then there was the start of recognition that simply building more freeways, or widening existing ones, was no ultimate solution; the city would just run out of space.

The County of Los Angeles, which covers the greater metropolitan area, is a conurbation of 84 cities (American designation), of which the city of Los Angeles is the largest, covering the central and north-west area. Once regarded as virtually slumless, the area is now not without its social problems (witness the notorious Watts riots of 1965), stemming in part from the high proportion of hispanics and blacks whose social opportunities are in marked contrast to the common perception of the area from its association with such suburbs as Beverley Hills. In 1964 the Southern California Rapid Transit District (RTD) was formed to take over the ailing private transit com-

▶A southbound train leaves Washington Boulevard station at the north end of the private right-of-way. Note the high platform station. _J. Wolinsky_

▶▼The median reservation of Washington Boulevard is protected by high concrete kerbs. _J. Wolinsky_

▼Entering Slauson Ave station this train is on a new elevated section which takes the light rail line over a busy road intersection and rail junction. _J. Wolinsky_

panies and operate a co-ordinated bus system across the county (some cities, such as Long Beach, provide municipal bus service). With operating subsidy and new investment a comprehensive network was maintained. An early and successful initiative was the El Monte busway, which reserved two exclusive lanes of the San Bernadino freeway for buses over a distance of 17.5 km, with a dedicated terminal at El Monte incorporating feeder bus transfers, park-and-ride, and from 1976, when High Occupancy Vehicles (carrying three or more persons) were permitted to use the lanes, a car-pooling staging post. Starting in 1973 with 3000 passenger trips/day, use of the busway built up to 18 000 trips/day.

Rail rapid transit was on the agenda; Los Angeles was the largest metropolitan area in the world, yet had no such a facility. The Los Angeles County Transportation Commission (LACTC) started rail planning in the 1970s as soon as it was formed, but voters rejected a massive plan to superimpose rail rapid transit on the freeway network in 1974. The turning point was the 1980 referendum which approved Proposition A, raising the sales tax in the county by 0.5% to provide funds for rail transit, city transit projects and bus fare reductions. The collection of Proposition A revenues began in 1982, after the state Supreme Court ruled against a challenge to the validity of the tax. 25% of receipts is returned to local communities for their own transit improvements, 35% is earmarked for the rail transit programme and the balance was used initially to provide a 50 cent bus fare for three years (which increased patronage by 40%). In order to have more funding up front, future tax revenues from this source have been used to guarantee revenue bonds issued to finance capital projects.

Proposition A identified 240 km in 13 broad corridors with the potential for rail transit.In early 1982 LACTC chose Los Angeles–Long Beach as the corridor for its starter line, ironically the last Pacific Electric rail line in 1961. This was selected

on the basis of cost, right-of-way availability and potential patronage. By 1983 conventional light rail had been chosen as the most cost-effective way of providing the service and six alternative routeings were under evaluation. At the same time five more high priority corridors were adopted. By combining these with the Wilshire Metro Rail starter line (a heavy rapid transit underground line linking Union Station with North Hollywood, under construction with a combination of local and federal finance), the Long Beach line, and the El Monte and Harbor busways, a complete network was defined with an overall performance better than the sum of the individual parts.

Selection of a second light rail line came in 1984, when the decision was taken that a proposed interim busway in the median strip of the new Century Freeway should be built as a 27 km light rail line from the outset at a cost of US$ 391 million. The Century Freeway, which runs east-west through the southern part of the county from the airport (LAX) to Norwalk, was a contested project which received a consent decree in 1981 only with the requirement that a transit facility be incorporated into the median. Subsequently the alignment of an extension of the light rail line from LAX south to El Segundo was agreed.

By 1985 the selected route of the Long Beach line was determined, and the environmental impact statement completed, so that construction of the US$ 595 million 35 km line could be authorised to start. The original intention to build a simple

▼ An interior view of the 2.65-m wide car showing the 2+2 seating and wide gangway through the articulation. *G. Nishio*

▲ The first car to arrive in Los Angeles on a test run on private right-of-way near Wardlow Road. *J. Wolinsky*

◄ Before being shipped to the USA one of the cars was exhibited in the US Pavilion at a Japanese exhibition. *G. Nishio*

line on the San Diego model was changed after the patronage and capacity studies, and the approved project included an 800 m subway at the Los Angeles end (which would include an interchange station with the heavy metro, now known as the Red Line, and due to open in early 1994), segregation of street-running sections, double-track throughout and high platforms at each stop for level boarding and alighting. Construction work started in 1986 for completion of the basic line in summer 1990; the Long Beach loop would take a little longer, and the subway 12–18 months longer due to delays in building the interchange station. In 1987, after competitive tendering, a US$ 69.6 order for 54 six-axle articulated LRVs was placed with the American subsidiary of the Japanese Sumitomo company, in association with Japanese car builder Nippon Sharyo. This order included 31 cars for the Long Beach line and 23 for the Century line.

In 1988 the LACTC accepted consultants recommendations that the Century Line lent itself to advanced technology with automatic train control and (since the line was completely segregated) third rail current collection. Thus it seemed the line would emerge as something like the Docklands Light Railway or Vancouver Skytrain. This was expected to add US$ 23 million to the cost of the project, and meant that the rolling stock ordered would not be suitable. Within a year the Commissioners were regretting their decision, as cost estimates for the automated line escalated by US$ 240 million, and a re-evaluation of the project led to a decision to use overhead current collection for greater compatibility with the Long Beach line (in particular shared depot facilities). However 28 automated cars would be ordered for the Norwalk–El Segundo line (now designated as the Green Line), with the hope that private finance would meet some of the cost. Construction work has started for completion in 1994. The first light rail cars for the Los Angeles–Long Beach line (now the Blue Line) were delivered in June 1989, permitting work to start on training 40 RTD bus drivers to drive the LRVs.

The third corridor to receive attention was that linking the central area of Los Angeles with Pasadena. Route and technology evaluations took place in 1989–90 and it was determined that the corridor should be built as a US$ 688 million, 21.6 km extension of the Blue Line from Flower St to Pasadena along the Santa Fe railway right-of-way through the north-eastern part of Los Angeles, with completion in 1998. The 54 Japanese cars would provide a combined fleet for the Long Beach and Pasadena lines. More recently work has started on the evaluation of a proposal for a Blue Line branch from Washington Boulevard to the Coliseum Sports Stadium and University of Southern California, which would be the terminus of trains from Pasadena. This would be capable of further extension to Culver City and Santa Monica. Extensions of the Green Line to be looked at are from El Segundo to Torrance, and a branch to Marina del Rey. At the eastern end the adjacent Orange County is considering rail transit for the corridor served by the former Pacific Electric alignment to Santa Ana. Another corridor under evaluation for light rail is Los Angeles–Glendale, which could eventually become the northern terminus of service from Long Beach.

Future progress with these schemes will be aided not just by Proposition A funds, but also by the June 1990 California state referendum which approved three more propositions for transit funding. Thus petrol tax will be doubled over the next five years, a further US$ 1000 million in bonds will be issued to finance transit and inter-city rail proposals, and there will be a US$ 1990 million bond issue for a specific set of rail and transit projects. This remarkable volte-face by the voters over the course of the last 20 years has been prompted largely by environmental considerations. The Los Angeles basin in particular has been notorious for its smog for 30 years, but only more recently has the realisation of the effect of this on health and the environment expressed itself in a willingness to tackle the motorisation that is largely responsible. The regional Air

Quality Board has voted to adopt a drastic plan to curb what is recognised as the worst air pollution in the USA, caused by 5.6 million cars and 2 milion commercial vehicles. In addition to higher registration and parking fees, this includes the adoption of clean fuels, electric buses on all routes with headways of 15 minutes or less, and 435 km of rail transit and commuter rail lines. The specific Los Angeles area proposals to benefit from the 1990 propositions include extensions of the Red Line, a 21 km connecting rail transit line in the San Fernando valley from Universal City to Warner Center, a 24 km coast corridor north–south line linking with the Green Line at El Segundo, eastward extension of the Green Line by 4 km to Norwalk rail station, the Pasadena line, and commuter rail service from Los Angeles to San Bernadino, Saugas, Ventura, San Clemente and San Diego.

In the meantime Los Angeles commuters can sample what light rail means to them, with the official opening of service on the Blue Line on 14th July 1990. A fortnight of free travel was followed by revenue service from 1st August, and inauguration of the Long Beach loop on 1st September until 14th February 1991. Shuttle buses work from the Pico Boulevard station at the subway ramp along Flower St to 7th St. 15 two-car trains run every 10 minutes at peaks, 10 every 15 minutes off-peak, with service from 05.00 to 21.00 daily. The timetabled journey time is 55 minutes. There is a flat fare of US$ 1.10, paid at platform ticket machines. An additional 25 cents purchases a transfer to a bus route. There is a 60 cent local fare in Long Beach. About 675 000 passengers sampled the line during the free fare period; revenue loadings built up to 19 000 passengers/day by the end of August, with the millionth passenger carried 40 days after inauguration. Emphasising the intention to maintain total security on a line with unmanned stations that passes through some of Los Angeles's worst gangland, the RTD has a two-year US$ 20 million contract with the Sheriff's Department to provide 118 deputies to ride and patrol the line.

The out-turn cost of the line was US$ 877 million, US$ 41 million over budget after allowing for inflation, but US$ 67 million had to be spent to move a freight railway in Compton in order to gain the community's agreement to the project, and this was not in the original budget. A breakdown of the main cost headings is as follows:

US$ million

civil engineering	324
professional services	188
rolling stock	79
land acquisition	58
communications system	49
insurance	37
electrification	34
trackwork	33
depot	33

Projected revenue for the first year is US$ 26.4 million, compared with operating costs of US$ 27.7 million.

The line is managed by RTD from a central control centre located at Imperial Ave/Wilmington Ave, close to the intersection with the future Green Line, which will also be controlled from here. All systems, including ticket machines, are monitored by a computer system. The depot and maintenance facility is in north Long Beach, by the intersection of the light rail line with the freeway and Union Pacific railway. The yard can accomodate up to 90 cars, and the maintenance shop 15. There is a separate paint shop. The depot serves as home base for all the operating personnel, who work a two-shift system.

So the city of the motorcar has succumbed to the advantages of the tram for second time in its history. The new rail era in Southern California seems set to be as significant as the last, albeit for different reasons, and sets the pace for others to follow.

LOS ANGELES *METRO RAIL PLAN*

LACTC

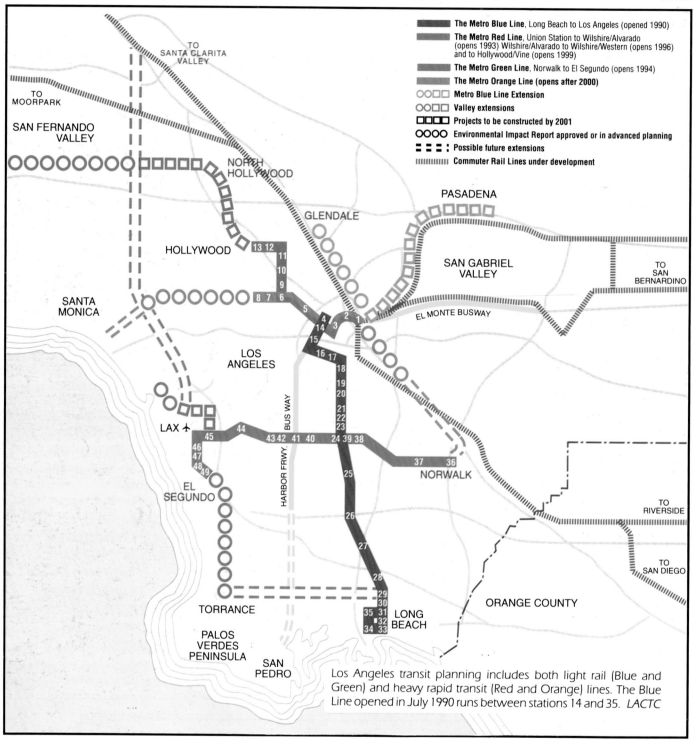

The **Metro Blue Line**, Long Beach to Los Angeles (opened 1990)
The **Metro Red Line**, Union Station to Wilshire/Alvarado (opens 1993) Wilshire/Alvarado to Wilshire/Western (opens 1996) and to Hollywood/Vine (opens 1999)
The **Metro Green Line**, Norwalk to El Segundo (opens 1994)
The **Metro Orange Line** (opens after 2000)
OOO□□ Metro Blue Line Extension
OO□□□ Valley extensions
□□□□ Projects to be constructed by 2001
OOOO Environmental Impact Report approved or in advanced planning
= = = Possible future extensions
|||||||||| Commuter Rail Lines under development

Los Angeles transit planning includes both light rail (Blue and Green) and heavy rapid transit (Red and Orange) lines. The Blue Line opened in July 1990 runs between stations 14 and 35. *LACTC*

STATION LOCATIONS

Metro Red Line-*Union Station to Hollywood/Vine*
1. Union Station
2. 1st St./Hill St. (Civic Center)
3. 5th St./Hill St.
4. 7th St./Flower St.
5. Wilshire Blvd./Alvarado St.
6. Wilshire Blvd./Vermont Ave.
7. Wilshire Blvd./Normandie Ave.
8. Wilshire Blvd./Western Ave.
9. Vermont Ave./Beverly Blvd.
10. Vermont Ave./Santa Monica Blvd.
11. Vermont Ave./Sunset Blvd.

12. Hollywood Blvd./Western Ave.
13. Hollywood Blvd./Vine St.

Metro Blue Line-*Long Beach to Los Angeles*
14. 7th St./Flower St.
15. Pico Blvd./Flower St.
16. Grand Ave./Washington Blvd.
17. San Pedro St./Washington Blvd.
18. Washington Blvd./Long Beach Ave.
19. Vernon Ave./Long Beach Ave.
20. Slauson Ave./Long Beach Ave.
21. Florence Ave./Graham Ave.
22. Firestone Blvd./Graham Ave.
23. 103rd St./Graham Ave.

24. Imperial Hwy./Wilmington Ave.
25. Compton Blvd./Willowbrook Ave.
26. Artesia Blvd./Acacia Ave.
27. Del Amo Blvd./Santa Fe Ave.
28. Wardlow Rd./Pacific Ave.
29. Willow St./Long Beach Blvd.
30. Pacific Coast Hwy./Long Beach Blvd.
31. Anaheim St./Long Beach Blvd.
32. 5th St./Long Beach Blvd.
33. 1st St./Long Beach Blvd.
34. 1st St./Pine Ave.
35. 5th St./Pacific Ave.

Metro Green Line-*Norwalk to El Segundo*
36. Studebaker Rd./605 Fwy.

37. Lakewood Blvd./Imperial Hwy.
38. Long Beach Blvd./Imperial Hwy.
39. Imperial Hwy./Wilmington Ave.
40. Avalon Blvd./117th St.
41. 110 Fwy./117th St.
42. Vermont Blvd./117th St.
43. Crenshaw Blvd./119th St.
44. Hawthorne Blvd./111th St.
45. Aviation Blvd./Imperial Hwy.
46. Mariposa Ave./Nash St.
47. El Segundo Ave./Nash St.
48. Douglas St.
49. Freeman Ave.

PHOTO FEATURE
Europe 1990

▲Stuttgart continues its programme of up-grading metre-gauge tramways to standard-gauge light rail lines. In November 1990 the route up the Weinsteige hill to the south-eastern suburbs was converted with a new alignment mostly in tunnel, but including an open station for the famous view over the city. On a test run in May two Stadtbahn cars are seen at the new station while a tram passes on the highway alignment in the background.   *B. Koehl*

►The Rheinbahn transport undertaking in Düsseldorf has pioneered the construction of the aluminium-bodied version of the Stadtbahn-B design of light rail car, reducing unladen weight from 43.4 to 38.4 tonnes. This example is seen in the tram and pedestrian precinct in the neighbouring town of Neuss.   *W. J. Wyse*

►November 1990 saw the opening of the Amstelveen line in Amsterdam, blending tramway, light rail and metro operation on one corridor. High-floor sneltram cars built by BN provide a fast service to the city centre via the metro, and are equipped for operation using overhead current collection in Amstelveen and third-rail current collection in the metro.   *P. Trotter*

◄ Romania has built seven new tramway systems in the last decade as part of a programme to boost electric city transport. This home-built double-ended car serves new housing development in Bucuresti. *E. Lassbacher*

► The reunited city of Berlin is still struggling to weld together two disparate public transport systems. It seems as if the modernised tramways of East Berlin, exemplified by this Tatra set in Hans-Beimler-Strasse, will be extended into West Berlin.
F. W. Schneider III

◄ The Austrian city of Graz has adopted a policy of expanding its tramway system to provide a high-quality service. As well as second-hand articulated trams from Germany, these new six-axle cars have been delivered by SGP, introducing a new corporate identity.
M. Moerland

► The Trondheim tramways were re-opened in August 1990 under the new ownership of a private company, reversing the previous action of the city council in replacing trams with buses in 1988. Seven of the 11 articulated trams built eight years ago have been taken over by GKB. *R. Kirchbahn*

◄ A home product from the Italian Firema company that is building the Manchester Metrolink vehicles is these articulated cars for Roma's suburban ACOTRAL tramway.
P. Gregoris

CONFERENCE REPORT

Light Rail Transit: Progress and Implementation 1990

by Michael Ballinger

On 23rd May, 1990, Aston University, Birmingham, held its third conference on light rail transit, this year concentrating on progress and implementation in 1990.

Roger Hall, Project Executive of Greater Manchester Passenger Transport Executive, gave the first paper, which reviewed recent progress with the Manchester Metrolink project. In the previous six months the emphasis had shifted to the preparation and agreement of the contracts for the design, construction and operation of this system; this had led to what the speaker described as a field day for the accountancy and legal professions. It was not simply a case of the Greater Manchester PTE and the chosen consortia settling one simple agreement: other bodies such as British Rail, the Metropolitan Borough Councils and the statutory undertakings (water, gas, electricity, telephone) each had to have their interests protected as well, and this had led to a multitude of separate contracts being necessary. Furthermore these agreements had to take into account future events that may require modification to methods of operation – for example changes to legislation once the system is running.

Construction work had started prior to the final signing of these contracts. The first tangible evidence of the project being underway was the diversion of the various utilities, and this alone had cost in the region of £7 million. As with the contractual stage, it was necessary to take into account possible future events, such as extensions to the system; some works for the future Salford Quays/Trafford Park lines had been incorporated in British Rail works at Cornbrook Junction. The first section of city-centre trackwork had recently been commenced near Victoria Station, and site preparation for the depot and control centre was under way.

At the same time that Phase 1 was being implemented, the PTE was looking to the future and examining possible extensions, with special reference to cost, patronage and revenue. The main problem with these extensions will be raising the funds to meet the capital cost, since considerable private finance will be necessary.

Mr Hall expressed a view that more vehicles would be needed once the system was operating, but it would be a problem to fund these from the operating revenue. On a wider basis, he was unsure whether the design/build/operate type of contract was the most suitable method of approaching such projects, and he felt that further examination of this idea is needed.

Jim Steer, of consultants Steer, Davis & Gleave, followed this with a starkly realistic approach to the possibility of implementing LRT in the UK. He identified three fundamental questions:

● Why light rail transit?
● Is it practical (particularly in funding terms) to build LRT?
● Will major local interests come together or disagree over the project?

If it was possible to pass these hurdles, five further key questions needed to be answered:

● Should LRT operate through pedestrian precincts in the urban centres, and if not was there an alternative (given that funding was unlikely to permit subway construction)?

● Are there roads available with excess capacity in the present and the future?
● Are there other natural routes?
● Do these last two points correspond with the corridors of demand?
● Is there space for a depot, park-and-ride, and kiss-and-ride facilities, and what will be the response of local residents?.

The speaker reviewed the various sources of funding, and advised LRT promoters attempting to attract finance from developers not to identify alignments until the last possible moment. This would help to build up competition between developers, and thus create a scenario whereby the maximum funding from developers could be attracted to the scheme. He quoted as an example the Docklands extension of the Jubilee line (see the editorial in Modern Tramway magazine for August 1990).

Howard Potter, formerly Head of Transport Planning of the London Docklands Development Corporation, then reviewed the planning and development of the Docklands Light Railway. Unfortunately this subject had been well covered over the last three years and his presentation was less informative than Jon Willis' paper presented to the 1989 conference (see Light Rail Review 1), which showed where the planners had gone wrong! Mr Potter stated that what had been wanted was a "high-tech" system, showing a slide of Utrecht as an example of what the LDDC had not wanted. At least the mobility impaired and mothers with push chairs do not have to rely on unreliable lifts to gain access to the Utrecht system!

Geoff Smith of Centro (the West Midlands PTE) covered the West Midlands scene before describing the organisation that had been necessary to get the Midland Metro project to its present state; as with the first speaker, delegates were made aware of the considerable amount of work necessary to implement a light rail scheme.

The main part of this paper related to the funding assessment of line 1. A nine-month project had been undertaken to identify the work required to meet the section 56 criteria. Specific computer simulation models had been developed to help, and the VIPS model could predict the number of public-transport passenger transfers to light rail. To predict transfers by motor car users, consultants had developed a modal split model. Other models looked at the effect on highways in the corridor, labour supply and economic regeneration benefits.

From these estimates, transport benefits had included time savings accruing to road users, vehicle operating cost savings, and accident operating-cost savings, over a 30-year period. This evaluation included not just the effects of the metro, but also took into account such projects as new roads to be built in the Black Country and the reinstatement of the Galton Junction–Snow Hill railway line. Other benefits included an assessment of deferred capital and reduced maintenance costs for roads, and savings in tendered bus operations. The total of these non-user transport benefits was estimated to be almost £71 million.

Other non-user, but non-transport, benefits fell into four categories:

● Property value enhancement.
● Employment benefits (both in the construction of the system and the regeneration it would prompt).
● Environmental benefits.
● Accessibility to town centres.

Other (but harder to quantify) benefits exist, such as the intensification of activity in urban areas and consequent saving of greenfield sites, and general improvements to the overall image of the region. All these benefits were estimated to total about £54 million.

The capital costs of line 1 had been revised to a 1989 base level of £73.2 million, including £12 million for 10 vehicles, land purchase, landscaping and project management costs. Operating costs of £2.17 million/year compared favourably with estimated revenue in the range £3.36–£4.42 million, generated from 6.31–8.21 million trips.

Centro was also investigating sources of finance other than central government grant, to reduce reliance on Section 56 funding, and consultants had been appointed to undertake this, whilst at the same time defining an appropriate company structure.

Finally the speaker identified the steps for the successful implementation of a transit scheme:

● Identify needs.
● Select appropriate solution.
● Develop the scheme in detail.
● Attract support from politicians and the public.
● Develop planning and organisation.

These needed commitment and determination.

After lunch it was the turn of the academics. Paul Truelove first examined the relationship of the suburban railway to light rail, with special reference to the West Midlands. He identified that for longer distances, heavy rail would be more attractive to people who would otherwise use cars, and he anticipated that buses would be more attractive to short-distance riders because of their closer stop spacing.

He also wondered if the the £140 million Black Country Spine Road would affect Midland Metro line 1, although as mentioned earlier this had been taken into account when the light rail project was evaluated. His idea of a veritable network of new roads in the area was just 24 hours too early; by the following day the £140 million had risen to £200 million, and the project was called in for ministerial review.

Barry Simpson completed the list of speakers with a comparison of some West European examples of metros and tramways. Research undertaken by himself and students at Aston University on the reaction of the public and businesses to rapid transit systems in Marseille, Lyon, Lille, Nantes and Grenoble were of interest, and showed positive support for such projects. Attempting to show that claims of LRT inspiring development are overstated, he showed a slide of La Cuire on Lyon metro line C, stating that he could see no sign of development having taken place in this area (a point he had made the previous year). But this contention failed to take into account the primary role of rapid transit, i.e. to get people to and from urban centres rather than fulfill a role more appropriate to a peoplemover system by linking major developments.

The main conclusion of this conference was that in the UK of the 1990s, planning must be concentrated on how a system was to be funded. Time and again speakers referred to the rules for Section 56 Grants. However in the open forum that followed the conference, perhaps the most interesting question was posed by consultant Robert Crawford, who asked what studies had been carried out to develop systems, and especially vehicles, that were inherently user-friendly. Some evidence from the conference could indicate that this was sometimes only the last factor to be considered in planning LRT. It could be a useful topic for a future conference.

▲ The fact that there has been no dramatic development around the Henon and Cuire stations of Lyon light metro line C does not mean that the line has not justified its construction. In practice it is a vital link for the residents of this hilly area to reach the main metro system and the city centre. *TCL*

LIGHT RAIL TRANSIT
Current Developments in the United Kingdom

by Michael Taplin

Although the first of the new wave of British light rail schemes, the partly street-based Manchester Metrolink, is not yet in public service, interest in light rail as a solution to both transport and inner-city problems has never been higher. This is because local politicians realise that if their city centres are to remain civilised places to live, work and shop, the apparently inexorable growth in motor traffic must be contained. The highway networks in these urban areas cannot be extended or adapted to cater for the predicted doubling of traffic levels by the year 2005, and even if they could the environmental consequences would be quite unacceptable.

In the short term it may be possible to achieve some improvement in public transport using buses and bus priority measures. However even with bus lanes and priorities such as traffic signal pre-emption, buses will become more and more susceptible to the increasing highway congestion, and any success they do have in increasing public transport flows will mean that eventually they will not be the most cost-effective method of meeting those flows. Making buses behave like trams by putting them on tracks (guided buses) is another idea being canvassed; this does little for the economic argument. for each bus still requires a driver and has to be replaced at least twice as frequently as a tram, while there is still a track cost and the need to obtain authorising powers.

It can be argued that it will be difficult to entice back to buses those car drivers who gave up the bus for a "superior" form of personal transport in the past. Although diesel buses may be a "cleaner and greener" solution to environmental problems than the private car, they still create pollution at the point of service delivery.

Thus the potential for light rail transit has moved beyond the major conurbations. It is seen to have the flexibility to fit into a wide variety of urban situations, attract more patronage than buses, be capable of cost-effective implementation and operation, and make a significant contribution towards urban regeneration and the protection of the environment. Its ability to influence the modal split between private and public transport in favour of the latter is seen as a key to relieving traffic congestion.

Of course each case will need to be examined on its merits, and careful economic assessment must go hand in hand with the engineering and operating studies that are necessary to make a valid case. Sufficient of these studies have now been carried out, by a variety of eminent consultants, to show that the arguments in favour of light rail are neither spurious nor subjective. However, light rail has a high initial cost, and makes therefore a significant call on scarce financial resources in both the public and private sectors.

Unfortunately central government has so far shown little inclination to produce the redistribution of funding that will be necessary to permit more than one scheme per year to be authorised for funding. The House of Commons Transport Committee hearing evidence on light rail were told that expenditure of £500 million per year (20% of that in the trunk road programme) would permit progress on those schemes which were most advanced.

Nevertheless, when HM Treasury does permit urban public transport outside London to receive its fair share of the national cake, either under this or another government, there will be no shortage of schemes awaiting approval. Fortunately work is already in progress to replace the private Bill procedure with something more appropriate to present needs, so at least the Parliamentary log jam should be avoidable in future.

Progress achieved on existing and new light rail schemes since publication of Light Rail Review 1 is described below.

BLACKPOOL

Britain's surviving tramway continues to hold its own with seafront and Fleetwood traffic, despite bus competition, but the undertaking faces a major problem of fleet replacement if it is to upgrade its service in any significant way. Eight modern single-deck trams may be enough to provide the basic winter service, but the pre-war single and double-deck cars that shift the crowds from Easter to November will have to be replaced at some time. Efforts to bring in a Tatra tram on demonstration from Czechoslovakia in 1990 were put on hold, ironically when the Czech firm signed a collaboration agreement with the British rolling stock company BREL.

TYNE & WEAR

The Metro marked its 10th anniversary in August 1990. Construction of the 3.5 km £12 million extension from Kenton Bank Foot to Newcastle Airport started in June 1990, for completion in late 1991, with passenger service in early 1992. Funding is coming from the PTA (money from the sale of its bus company) and a grant from the airport company. The extension will be operated from within existing rolling stock resources, taking up some of the slack brought about by bus deregulation (which reduced annual passengers from 58 to 50 million). A study is in progress to evaluate routes and financing opportunities for a Metro extension to Washington and Sunderland, with recommendations expected in Spring 1991.

A group of local businessmen, with the backing of Gateshead Metropolitan Borough, have commissioned a study for an 11 km tramway along the south bank of the Tyne from the centre of Gateshead to the Metro Centre (a giant retail development), then south to serve leisure developments in the Derwent Valley. Second-hand continental trams would be used.

LONDON

Docklands Light Railway. With the railway already carrying 33 000 passengers/day (compared with the original forecast of 22 000 by 1992), work continues on a major upgrading to meet the higher traffic levels expected when the extensions to Bank (the heart of the City of London) and Beckton are opened in summer 1991 and early 1993 respectively, and the financial centre at Canary Wharf is completed. 10 new cars were delivered by BREL in 1990, and delivery of 44 from BN in Belgium is scheduled to start in January 1991. A further 26 BN cars has been ordered for 1992 delivery at a cost of £20 million. Consideration is being given to the future of the original 11 cars, which are not fire-proofed to a standard that permits them to be used in the Bank tunnel; if a suitable offer were

forthcoming they may well be sold, thus retaining operational flexibility of the whole fleet. The existing automatic train operation system is to be replaced by the SELTRAC moving block system from Alcatel Canada. Current investment in DLR is of the order of £600 million and further developments are in the pipeline as detailed on pages 67–77.

Croydon. A final study is in progress to determine detailed route definition, environmental impact and operational plans for the proposed light rail network centred on this south London Borough, and public consultation has started. It is proposed to move towards deposit of a Bill in Parliament in November 1991. The cost estimate for the scheme, which includes conversion of British Rail lines, is £80 million. Later extensions could take the system to Sutton, Epsom and Beckenham. The London Borough of Merton have commissioned a study into the feasibility of converting the Wimbledon–Sutton rail line to light rail as an extension of this network.

Kingston. London Transport have carried out studies with the London Borough of Kingston covering conversion of the BR lines to Shepperton and Chessington South to light rail, with extension of the latter to Epsom, and street running between Kingston and Surbiton, at an estimated cost of £60 million. More detailed study is expected in 1991. There is the potential for a link between this scheme and the Croydon system at Epsom.

Watford. A joint study involving Hertfordshire County Council, London Transport and British Rail has considered light rail as one option for the extension of the Chesham LT line to Watford (where there would be a street link),and then on the existing BR line to St Albans. The alignment will be preserved pending further consideration.

Alexandra Palace. The London Borough of Haringey is commissioning a feasibility study for a light rail link between Tottenham, Wood Green and the refurbished Alexandra Palace, with the potential for extension to Highgate. Traditional trams would be used as a tourist attraction for the Alexandra Palace link.

Redbridge. The Borough Development Plan reserves the alignment of the former Seven Kings–Newbury Park railway for future transit use.

GREATER MANCHESTER

Construction work is in progress for the 32 km, £110 million, Metrolink line between Altrincham and Bury, including street operation through the centre of Manchester, where track laying commenced in June 1990. Full details are combined in a separate feature 'Metrolink Update'.

SOUTH YORKSHIRE

Parliamentary approval for the second light rail line, to Meadowhall in the Don Valley, was delayed by some archane political tactics unrelated to the merits of light rail, but Royal Assent finally came at the end of 1989, followed in 1990 by approval for a minor diversion of line 1 (Hillsborough–Mosborough). In February 1990 the Government announced that the whole scheme met its criteria for Section 56 grant, but that no funding was available to permit work to start in 1990. Thus there was no longer any possibility of operations starting in time for the World Student Games in Sheffield in 1991. On 11th December 1990, the government announced a 50% section 56 grant towards the £230 million scheme, and construction work will start in 1991 for completion of the first stage in 1993. The South Yorkshire scheme is the first to qualify for Section 56 grant under the revised criteria, and the equation which convinced the Department of Transport was as follows (indexed to 100):

Costs:	Capital cost	77.0
	Annual costs	27.0
	Developers contributions	4.0
	Net cost	100.0

Benefits:	User benefits captured as revenue	77.0
	Non-user benefits – decongestion	16.8
	employment impact	12.1
	savings on subsidised buses	2.2
	highway impacts	1.3
	accident reduction	0.6
	environmental	0.6
	Total revenue + non-user benefits	110.6

Cost/benefit ratio 110.6 over 100 = 1.1

In anticipation of this favourable funding decision, the PTE had already issued letters of intent to contractors for the construction of the system (Balfour Beatty) and the rolling stock (Siemens/Duewag). Rolling stock will be a specially-designed eight-axle articulated car with all axles motored, and low-floor sections behind the bogies of the outer body sections.

WEST MIDLANDS

The first line of the proposed Midlands Metro (Birmingham–Wolverhampton) received Royal Assent in November 1989, and an application for Section 56 funding towards the anticipated £73 milion cost is at present being evaluated by the Department of Transport. The Section 56 application identifies non-user benefits totalling £124.6 million. Tenders are being invited for a Build, Operate, Maintain concession on the Manchester model. Also in November 1989, two further Bills were deposited, for lines from Birmingham (Fiveways, and in subway under the city centre) to Castle Bromwich and the National Exhibition Centre/Airport (26 km) and between Wolverhampton, Walsall and Dudley (26 km); these remain under consideration by Parliament, but have passed the Opposed Bills Committee.

Bills were deposited in November 1990 for extension of the Dudley line to the Merry Hill retail and business centre in Brierley Hill and for a street loop in Wolverhampton, while work continues to evaluate possible alignments on to Stourbridge. Potential corridors in Coventry being evaluated for a 1991 Bill include a route from the city centre to Binley, with possible extension to Willenhall, and a route from the city centre to Canley for Tile Hill and Warwick University.

AVON

The privately-promoted light rail scheme for the Bristol area has made slow progress in the last year due to further political controversy. Bills were submitted in November 1989 to extend the original Portishead line from Wapping Wharf across the city centre to Temple Meads BR station, and from Temple Meads to Bradley Stoke and Yate. The city centre Bill initially failed to receive the required consent from the City Council, but this block was lifted in June and both Bills are now proceeding, with Committee consideration scheduled for Spring 1991.

In recognition of the need to work closely with the local authorities (particularly as public funding in the form of Section 56 grant was applied for in October 1990, and a matching local contribution will now be needed to finance the £192 million project), promoters ATA have signed a joint venture agreement with Avon County Council, and a joint project team has been established to progress the scheme. One consequence of this is that a consultation exercise has been carried out for alternative routes through east Bristol to meet concern at the effect of ATA proposals on the pedestrian/cycle path along the former railway alignment selected for use. An environmental assessment has been published for public comment. ATA are also seeking to establish potential alignments for 1991 Bills, including south Bristol, Avonmouth and Severn Beach, a Filton spur, Bristol to Bath and within Bath. The local bus company has taken a stake in ATA and is the nominated operator of the system, which will require 45 vehicles initially. Late news is that ATA have withdrawn the Bill for the Temple Meads–Bradley Stoke/Yate sections, to permit reconsideration of the route through the Bristol Development Corporation area.

WEST YORKSHIRE

Following withdrawal of the PTE Bill for light rail lines bet-ween the city centre and East Leeds, the City Council under-took its own study for an automated guideway line across the city from Seacroft to Middleton. However this project also generated considerable controversy and a joint transportation study is now in progress to evaluate all the possible options for fixed-track public transport serving Leeds, including light rail, automated mini-metro and guided bus. Preliminary results suggest light rail and a guided busway for a November 1991 Bill.

SOUTHAMPTON

The City Council Bill for an automated guideway line around the central area has met opposition in Parliament and is un-likely to be passed in the near future. In the meantime efforts continue to attract private funding to the project.

SOUTH HAMPSHIRE

The £65 million plans for a 11.2 km light rail line from Fareham to Gosport, and then by immersed tube under the harbour to Portsmouth, have been taken up for promotion by a consor-tium (South Hants Metro Ltd) formed by the local bus operator, the ferry company and construction company Farr Plc. The line is estimated to carry 40 000 passengers/day. Hampshire County Council is continuing its involvement in the project, in particular financing a study of criteria for Section 56 funding.

CLEVELAND

The Teesside Development Corporation and Cleveland County Council have progressed studies for light rail in the Darlington–Saltburn corridor to the point where public consul-tation is in progress on a core line between Stockton and Middlesbrough, with alternative extensions to Hardwick, Yarm, Ormesby, Ingleby Barwick and Coulby Newham. Costs are in the range £50–60 million and it is hoped to develop a firm proposal for submission to Parliament in November 1991.

NOTTINGHAM

Further work to identify city centre options for the £50 million, 12 km Hucknall–Midland Station light rail line has been car-ried out, and on-street operation across the city centre has been identified to be technically feasible, as well as reducing capital costs by £12 million. An awareness campaign has started to inform the public about the project, and it is hoped that approval can be obtained for a Bill to be deposited in November 1991.

EDINBURGH

After a two-year study of public transport options Lothian Regional Council announced plans for a light rail sysem with an 18 km north–south line (Muirhouse/Davidsons Main–Kaimes/Gilmerton via a city centre subway, including in part an abandoned rail tunnel) as the first phase, with an estimated cost of £184 million. A second east–west route linking Wester Hailes and Leith has been developed, estimated to cost £144 million. The studies are notable in involving the Scottish Office as part of an overall transportation study for Edinburgh. Evalu-ation of public consultation is taking place and it is hoped that a Bill can be deposited in November 1991.

GLASGOW

Strathclyde PTE have carried out a two-year Public Transport Development Study which include investigation of the poten-tial for light rail. Options for fully and partially-segregated lines (including conversion of some BR lines) were identified and supported by public consultation, with a 12-route network estimated to cost £500 million. Further work is in progress to identify a first phase for implementation.

BELFAST

Northern Ireland Railways have put forward a plan for light rail development based on conversion of existing and disused rail alignments. Consultants are examining city centre options on behalf of the Northern Ireland Department of the Environ-ment.

CARDIFF

The Cardiff Bay Development Corporation have appointed consultants to examine light rail feasibility to link the city centre and central station to the docks redevelopment area.

LANCASTER–HEYSHAM

A study is being considered for a light rail link in the Lancaster–Morecambe–Heysham corridor.

LIVERPOOL

The Merseyside Development Corporation is investigating ways of regenerating the older docks area and has identified the potential for light rail on a north–south alignment between Sandhills and the Garden Festival site (the route of the former Overhead Railway) and to link the waterfront with the city centre. The PTE is understood to be examining light rail poten-tial for routes to the eastern suburbs.

CHESTER

A pre-feasibility study sponsored by City and County Councils examined the potential for light rail and reported favourably on two corridors. These are being examined further, together with other possible alignments, as part of a wider traffic and transportation study for the city.

DARTFORD

A feasibility study on light rail/guided busway applications in Dartford is nearing completion. It was commissioned by the District Council to look at linking a number of development proposals alongside the Thames.

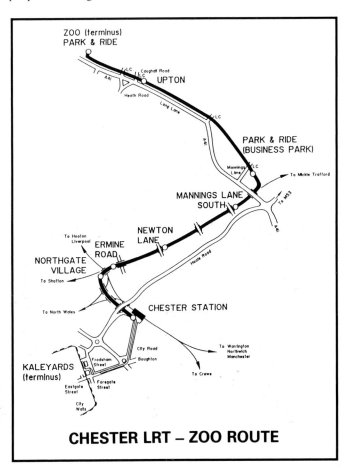

CHESTER LRT – ZOO ROUTE

READING

A Berkshire County Council study of rail potential in central Berkshire identified possible light rail opportunities and consultants recommended a £26 million 12.8 km system serving the Basingstoke and Bath Rd corridors. Further studies are planned.

SWINDON

Wiltshire County Council commissioned consultants for a transportation study that included evaluation of light rail potential, and identified opportunities for a viable system as an alternative to wholly road-based solutions. The results of public consultation are being considered.

GLOUCESTER & CHELTENHAM

A pre-feasibility study carried out by Gloucestershire County Council found there was potential for light rail in the Severn Vale area. Efforts are being made to form a consortium of public and private interests to finance a more detailed study. The British Waterways Board and Gloucester City Council are considering a heritage tramway to link the restored docks with the city centre.

PETERBOROUGH

The City Council is likely to commission a feasibility study into long-term light rail options.

CAMBRIDGE

The preparation of a new Cambridge Master Plan by the County Council included assessment of light rail proposals using existing or abandoned railway alignments, with a link to the city centre. A detailed study has identified a 15 km line from Oakington (former BR line to St Ives) to Trumpington (former BR line to Bedford), with 3.8 m on city streets, and a Parkway station for interchange with BR at Milton. It is hoped to take this forward as part of an overall traffic strategy that would include raising £70 million in funding from a computerised road congestion pricing scheme.

NORWICH

A major transportation study includes in its brief the examination of light rail options. Results are expected shortly.

GREAT YARMOUTH

A privately-sponsored 2.5 km light transit line (which would probably be built as a monorail) to serve tourist attractions along the sea front appears to be supported by the Borough Council, but has attracted initial opposition on from the County Council on planning and highway grounds.

BASILDON

A consortium have proposed an overhead guideway system for a 5 km link between the railway station and the new Astrodome complex.

SOUTHEND-ON-SEA

A general transportation study in progress includes investigation of the potential for rapid transit.

CHELMSFORD

The Chamber of Commerce and Borough Council have asked Essex County Council to consider a town centre peoplemover to link railway station, car parks and the shopping centre.

MEDWAY TOWNS

Kent County Council are carrying out a pre-feasibility study to examine the potential for light rail in Chatham, Rochester and Gillingham.

MAIDSTONE

A broad transportation study is expected to include evaluation of light rail potential, including a possible link with the Medway Towns scheme.

BRIGHTON

Preliminary consideration has been given to light rail, with consultants producing an outline proposal. A detailed study may follow.

BOURNEMOUTH

A general transportation study may include investigation of light rail options for the Bournemouth and Poole area.

PLYMOUTH

Consultants have recommended that light rail be evaluated as an option in the redevelopment of the waterside area, and the City and County Councils are to appoint consultants for a pre-feasibility study.

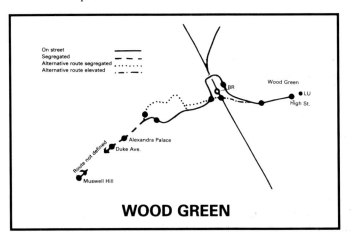

WOOD GREEN

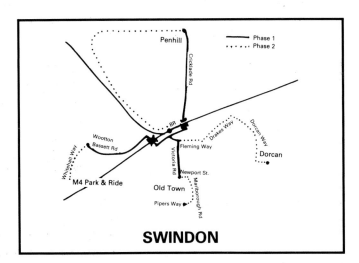

SWINDON

GUILDFORD

A feasibility study of alternative transport provision has been commissioned to include consideration of light rail options.

LUTON

The local bus operator have commissioned plans for future options in the Luton–Dunstable corridor, including the possibility of an 11-station light rail line.

BEDFORD

A study is in progress on new modes of passenger transit and will include evaluation of light rail as an option.

MILTON KEYNES

The City Council have commissioned a feasibility study of the potential for rapid transit in the area.

LEICESTER

Proposals for a north–south light rail line using abandoned railway alignment between Birstall and Narborough, with street running in the city centre, have been prepared by the County Council as part of an overall transportation strategy. A more detailed feasibility study is in progress.

DERBY

A tramway operation has been proposed by the City Council to serve pedestrian precincts in the central area.

POTTERIES

After an initial study of an elevated guideway system for the Stoke-on-Trent, Newcastle-under-Lyme and Hanley areas, a local authority working party is giving consideration to investigation of the potential for light rail.

HULL

Humberside County Council and the City Council commissioned consultants to examine options for various forms of light transit, with the results to be incorporated in a major transportation study for the area.

OTHER SCHEMES

Light transit options have been investigated in a preliminary way in Aberdeen, Dundee, Preston and Exeter, but not proceeded with. Besides the heritage tramway proposal at Gloucester already mentioned, there is a similar scheme in Swansea, where the bus company have investigated the re-opening of the Swansea to Mumbles line as a tourist attraction. This would depend on outside funding of half the £2 million cost, and at present this does not appear to be forthcoming.

Light transit also embraces a number of private systems that at present serve either airports or amusement parks. Gatwick airport features two examples of the Westinghouse guideway that is also being installed at Stanstead, while Birmingham airport is linked to the International rail station and National Exhibition Centre by the unique Maglev system. Monorails are features at Beaulieu Motor Museum, Blackpool Pleasure Beach and Alton Towers entertainment park.

A 2 km commercial monorail with a claimed capacity of 8 000 passengers/hour/direction has been built at a cost of £20 million to link car parks with retail and business centres at the Merry Hill complex at Brierley Hill, near Dudley, West Midlands. Commercial service has been delayed by several months due to the difficulty in securing railway inspectorate approval for the public operation because of concern over evacuation procedures from the elevated guideway.

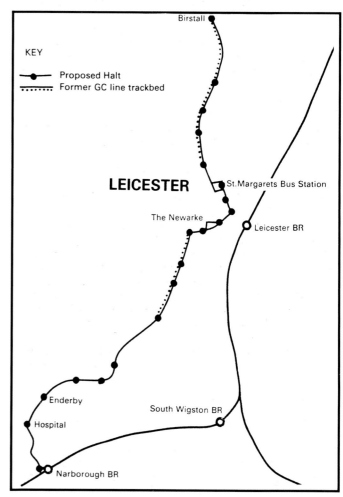

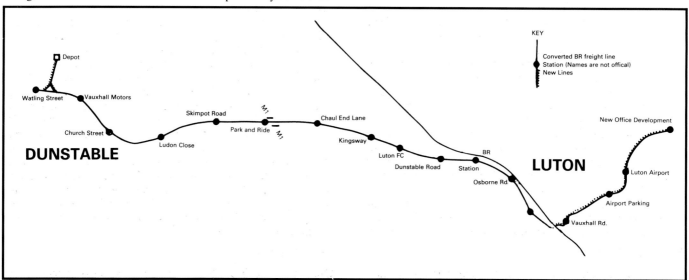

SYSTEM PLANNING
Light Rail for Nottingham
by Peter Fox

THE ZONE AND COLLAR SCHEME

In 1972 proposals for major road building in the centre of Nottingham were abandoned. It was proposed instead that a collar of traffic lights be placed around the city inside the ring road. At each traffic light-controlled point where a road entered the central area, there would be a lane for buses (and emergency vehicles) where flow was unrestricted, and a lane for cars. The flow on the car lane would be monitored and controlled by the traffic lights so that unacceptable levels of traffic could not build up in the central area. In residential zones outside the collar the flow onto the main arterial roads from the housing estates would also be controlled by traffic lights, again with a priority lane for buses. 'Park-and-ride' sites would be provided on these arterial roads and bus services in general would be increased in frequency. The system was tested on one segment on the west side of the city beginning in August 1975.

The experiment showed that, at that time, the system had little to offer and the infrastructure was dismantled. Analysis showed that over 90% of those driving into the town had a subsidised or free parking space available. Even with the 'collar' delays it was still considerably quicker to drive on into town than to park and change to a 'lilac leopard' (the coaches used on the park and ride service were lilac coloured Leyland Leopards). Attempts to artificially delay private cars merely resulted in the traffic queue tailing back past the entrance to the bus lane and were therefore self-defeating. The park-and-ride sites were very close to the central area; having driven that far, car drivers felt they may as well continue for the remaining 5 to 10 minutes to the office. There was minimal extra use of bus services. Although traffic was heavy at peak times, it flowed steadily. It was very much a solution looking for a problem!

THE PRESENT SITUATION

The picture is vastly different today. There is acute traffic congestion in morning and evening peaks, particularly on the west side of the city in the segment used for the experiment. The congestion stretches back more than 6 miles, such that movement in Long Eaton, for example, is exceedingly difficult between 8 am and 9 am due to traffic queuing on the road to Nottingham. A 7-mile journey can take over an hour. There is virtually no difference in journey time between bus and car, but the arrival times of the buses are quite unpredictable due to the varying effects of congestion from day to day. The lessons have not been learnt and the City Council still insists that developers of property in the city provide parking for a high proportion of their staff. Many council-owned parking spaces are rented out on annual contracts at rates which offer a large discount on the daily rates. There are still calls from councillors for more public parking to be provided in the city. Two park-and-ride sites now operate daily from about 7.30 am and are well-used. They are very close to the central area, however, and merely accommodate some of those who do not have a privileged parking space in the city.

It is clear from the above that a system which will see commuters leaving their cars not just outside the central area, but 6, 7 or 10 miles away (or even at home), is what is required now.

EARLY IDEAS FOR LRT

The first modern proposal for an LRT system in Nottingham was produced by Mr J.K. Chilvers in an MA thesis entitled 'A Rapid Transit System in Nottingham'. As the thesis was for an MA in architecture, after identifying a possible network of routes including a main north-south route which utilised the disused Great Central tunnels, it concentrated on aspects of the design of stations, vehicles and literature. Nevertheless, the possible network of routes examined are interesting when compared with the current proposals.

In particular, Chilvers investigated running the LRT system through the Victoria centre car park and concluded that although tight, it was possible providing third-rail current collection was used on that section.

THE PRESENT SCHEME

In March 1989, a joint study was commissioned by Nottinghamshire County Council, Nottingham Development Enterprise and Nottingham City Council to undertake a study of the feasibility of an LRT system for Greater Nottingham. This was carried out by Scott Wilson Kirkpatrick in association with Kennedy Henderson Ltd. and Peat Marwick McLintock. The main aims of the study were to:

● establish areas and key locations which an LRT system could feasibly serve
● formulate and assess route options and develop a plan for an LRT system and network of routes
● examine the engineering and transportation issues and potential patronage
● assess the likely contribution which the system could make to the regeneration of Greater Nottingham
● establish the likely cost of the initial route and examine ways in which it could be funded

Nineteen different routes were examined in five broad corridors of the Greater Nottingham area and these were reduced to six routes after evaluation based on such criteria as feasibility, construction costs, community acceptability, road congestion, patronage forecasts, regeneration impact and funding prospects.

Eventually, one route was selected for detailed study from Midland station to Hucknall with a branch line from Old Basford to Babbington where there would be a park-and-ride site near the M1 motorway.

Needless to say, other systems were examined including guided buses, trolleybuses, monorail and conventional rail, but light rail was found to be the most appropriate.

It was originally considered (naively in the opinion of the author) that the BR route from Lenton Jn. to Radford Jn. would be closed by BR to passenger traffic, leaving only trip freights to Calverton Colliery using the route. This would allow the proposed LRT system to use the route with a single BR line alongside. However, there was much opposition to this ridiculous closure proposal which would have increased the journey time from Sheffield to Nottingham by 6–10 minutes, and after a public inquiry in which BR were made to look silly by objectors, BR announced they were withdrawing the closure proposal and would divert all Sheffield–Nottingham trains along this route. Thus there was then no hope of the LRT system running this way.

THE OPTIONS

Once it was realised that it would not be possible to run via

Radford, the route from Nottingham Midland station was planned to use the abandoned Great Central Railway Viaduct and then the tunnels either side of the former Nottingham Victoria station, now occupied by a large shopping complex known as the Victoria Centre. The consultants' report concluded that it was not possible to pass through the Victoria Centre car park, due to lack of clearance and so that a new tunnel would have to be bored beneath the centre. On emerging from the tunnel, the route would turn west alongside the Forest recreation ground, thence via either of two different options to join the former Midland Railway route to Mansfield which is followed to the terminus at Hucknall. The Babbington branch uses the trackbed of the line to the now closed Babbington Colliery.

A further phase of the study has examined the possibility of running through the street in central Nottingham for the following reasons:

● To avoid the cost of the new Victoria Tunnel and hence make the project more financially viable.
● To make the LRT system more attractive to the public by a better penetration of the city centre.
● To assist the City Council in its desire to promote certain new shopping and commercial developments.

Three city centre options were examined as follows, all of which would leave the GCR viaduct just south of the former Weekday Cross Junction, and would end up at Upper Parliament Street.
OPTION A. This would run via Fletcher Gate, Victoria Street and South Parade.
OPTION B. Northbound as option A, but southbound via Smithy Row and Pelham Street.
OPTION C. Northbound along Low Pavement and Wheeler Gate, southbound as option A.

From Upper Parliament Street, the route would pass the popular Theatre Royal and run up Goldsmith Street and Waverley Street, continuing along the western edge of the Forest Recreation Ground on reserved track.

North of the Forest, the tunnel and street options both have a choice of routes to gain the MR route line, running either via Radford Road (northbound) and Noel Street (southbound) thence via Wilkinson Street, or via Gregory Boulevard and Alfreton Road (A610) to gain the MR route at Bobbers Mill Bridge.

THE ROBIN HOOD LINE

As well as the above LRT proposals, Nottinghamshire County Council along with other authorities are proposing to reopen the Nottingham–Mansfield–Worksop line to passenger traffic. Mansfield is the largest town in Great Britain without a railway station and its closure in 1964 was certainly ridiculous. The line was completely closed north of Annesley and was eventually cut back further. At present it exists as far as Linby, but is out-of-use north of Bestwood Park Jn., where the line to Calverton Colliery, used by around three return trip freights per day, diverges. The proposal involves reopening throughout, including reopening the filled-in Kirkby Tunnel, thence along a new alignment to join the freight route from the Midland Main Line at Pye Bridge to Mansfield and Worksop.

The Robin Hood Line uses the same route from Bobbers Mill or Wilkinson Street to Hucknall, but serves a different market. Only three stations are common to both schemes, and all can be used for interchange. As will be seen from the following section, if the LRT system were to be extended northwards to Mansfield, the journey time to Mansfield would be unacceptably long. Conversely, the BR line does not serve most of the districts that the LRT system does and is not planned to be high-frequency service.

THE CHOICES

Speed v. Access. The present name for the LRT system is 'Nottingham Rapid Transit'. This implies a fast system. From

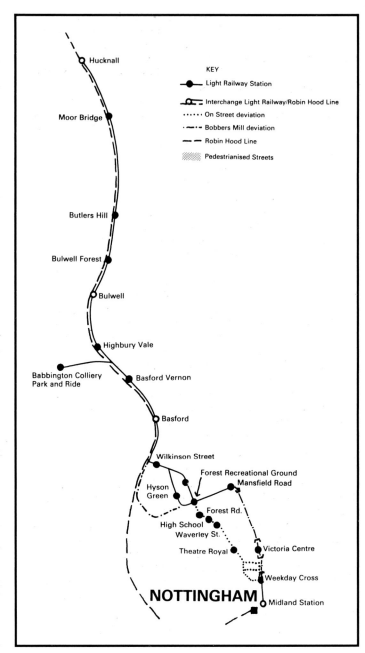

KEY
● — Light Railway Station
▭ — Interchange Light Railway/Robin Hood Line
⋯⋯ On Street deviation
-·-·- Bobbers Mill deviation
— — Robin Hood Line
▨ Pedestrianised Streets

NOTTINGHAM

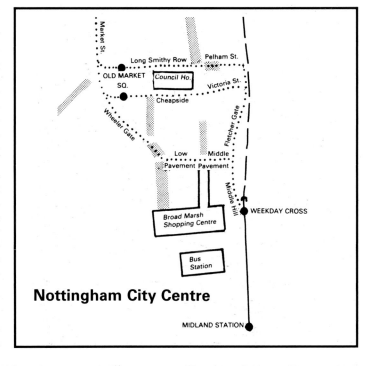

Nottingham City Centre

Hucknall to Nottingham Midland station, the tunnel option would take 25 minutes, whereas the street option would take 32 minutes. The obvious route which used to be available from Nottingham to Hucknall was the Great Central Railway alignment north of Victoria. This would have been considerably faster than either of the present options. Unfortunately, despite representations made in the past by pro-rail groups, the local authorities have allowed this route to be blocked by housing and industrial development – an extremely short-sighted policy which is now causing great problems.

The faster time by the tunnel route is, to some extent, offset by the time required to walk to the city centre, so the actual time difference to get to the Old Market Square, for example, would only be about two minutes.

The tunnel route is also more costly at £50.2 million, but the reduction in infrastructure costs associated with city centre street-running is to some extent offset by the fact that three extra cars are needed due to the increased journey time. The cars would also be more expensive, as the ruling gradient would be steeper. Nevertheless, the street option would only cost £42.3 million (£43.4 million via Bobbers Mill).

It would appear that the reduction in journey time gained by using the tunnel is not great enough to justify the increased cost, and that the improvement in city centre access more than compensates for any increased journey time. It may also be possible to reduce the journey time by appropriate traffic management measures.

It has recently been decided that the city centre route will be street-running with option A preferred. If it is not feasible to round the corner at Victoria Street because the curve is too tight, then option C would be used.

North of the Forest. The Radford Road/Noel Street option uses separate roads northbound and southbound to overcome the problem of the large amounts of traffic using Radford Road. Thus northbound the LRT route would be along Radford Road, whilst southbound Noel Street would be used. Noel Street is a narrow residential street with houses on both sides north of Berridge Road, but flanked by the supermarket site south of the junction. The street is wide enough to permit only two lanes of traffic and it is proposed that one of these would be used by all through traffic including LRVs. The other lane would be set aside for parking. North of Berridge Road the

street is one-way southbound.

The connection between Wilkinson Street and Noel Street, via Shipstone Street, a playground and Gladstone Street would raise conflict with other traffic in these constricted areas. This would necessitate the implementation of traffic management measures.

The Bobbers Mill option would connect with the BR line at Bobbers Mill Bridge, reached via Gregory Boulevard and Alfreton Road. Despite the generous width between building facades in the Boulevard, widening of the highway would be restrained by the mature trees which line it. The carriageway width would allow for two tracks of shared running with sufficient remaining either for waiting bays on one side, or for narrow lanes suitable for cyclists on both sides. An alternative provision for waiting would be the formation of short bays between the trees, which would be accommodated within the wide footways.

Alfreton Road carries heavy traffic in four lanes and any reduction in its capacity would have serious consequences. It would therefore be necessary to maintain the four-lane provision free of any interaction (except at junctions) with the LRT which would impede both the LRT operation and the traffic flow. This could only be achieved by land acquisition on both frontages of the road. There could be some demolition and some houses could lose part of their gardens. The LRT would take advantage of this widening by running on reserved tracks in the middle of, and for the length of, Alfreton Road.

It has now been decided the Radford Road/Noel Street option will be used, but that Noel Street will be used northbound and Radford Road southbound.

Alongside BR. Once the LRT system has joined the MR alignment, it is proposed that there would be four tracks (2 NRT and 2 BR), as far as Hucknall. This is possible for much of the distance, but there is a particular problem at Bulwell Bridge, where there is only room for two tracks. Whereas the Robin Hood line, with its 30-minute frequency, should have no problems in coping with a single line section, the NRT with a 5-minute frequency could experience delays when the time table is not strictly adhered to. If it were decided that NRT must have two tracks, then some street-running would have to take place in this area. One possibility is that NRT and BR trains could share tracks at this point. Much has been stated

▼The preferred option A in the city centre would have to go round this curve at the corner of Fletcher Gate and Victoria Street.
Peter Fox

▼If option A is not possible then trams would have to come down this steeply-graded road known as Low Pavement.
Peter Fox

about the incompatibility of LRT and heavy rail, particularly because the buffing heights are different, but with an effective system of ATP (automatic train protection), the two vehicles would effectively be prevented from ever coming into contact. Such a system is being employed in Karlsruhe (Nottingham's twin city!), and research carried out by British Rail Research for Regional Railways and the publicly expressed views of Major Holden of the Railway Inspectorate has now led BR to believe that such inter-running is a real option, provided that ATP is operative.

COST/BENEFIT ANALYSIS

Patronage forecasts were undertaken by Leeds University Institute of Transport studies. The results gave a prediction of 14 785 daily one-way journeys at a mean fare of around 47p resulting in a total daily revenue of £6,919, or £2.35 million per annum. The consultants estimated non-user benefits of between £26 and £45 million, depending on future economic trends. The table below gives the outline economic appraisal for the scheme, all figures being at 1989 prices.

	Present Value (£ million)	
COSTS		
Capital costs	36–43	(1)
Operating costs	16	
BENEFITS		
User benefits (revenue)	21	(2)
Non-user benefits:		
Congestion savings	26–45	
Development impact	6–9	(3)
Betterment effect	5–9	(4)
Job creation	3–5	

Notes:
(1) The total capital costs of the project have been assumed at roundly £50–60 million and, as construction was assumed to be from late 1992 to early 1994, the present value discounted at 8% per annum is £36–43 million.
(2) User benefits are less than would be expected from multiplying the annual figure by 30, as it is expected that patronage would build up gradually.
(3) Development impact occurs due to the likely increases in site values because of improved accessibility both to suburban sites in Babbington, Basford and Hucknall and in the city centre.
(4) Betterment effect is due to increase in values of existing properties.

Other non-user benefits which were not quantified during this appraisal but will require to be taken into account in an application for government funding are:

● Accident savings
● Savings in subsidies for tendered bus services.
● Environmental benefit.
● Reduction in the need for special subsidised services for the mobility impaired.

The economic appraisal above was based on the tunnel option. The effects of the alternative city centre street-running option have been detailed earlier.

PROJECT FUNDING

Funding for the construction of the LRT system (Infrastructure and equipment) may be obtained from three main sources;
● contributions from developers or owners of major sites which will benefit from improved access, or from major existing businesses located along the proposed LRT route
● moneys raised against the surplus of future revenues over the costs of operation of the railway
● funding from the public sector (local authorities, central government or European funding)
    The current approach of the Department of Transport is to expect promoters of LRT projects to raise the maximum contributions from developers and other beneficiaries of improved access, to use the operating surplus on the railway to raise private sector risk capital, and only thereafter to seek public sector funding for the remainder of the construction costs. The overall DTp criterion for justifying public sector funding of the project (from whatever source) is that the level of funding should be more than covered by 'non-user benefits' which it would be unreasonable to expect the promoter of the project to capture directly from the beneficiaries.
    Half of any public sector funding would be met directly by Section 56 grant from government and the remainder would be made available by increasing the local authority or PTE's credit approval, (as in the Sheffield case).
    A target figure for private developer contributions was set at £5 million. Unfortunately, this may prove to be overoptimistic; if developers think that the project will go forward anyway, they are apt to see no benefit in contributing themselves, so that any such contributions are likely to be only for enhancements of the system to benefit their particular vicinity.
    After allowing for an operating surplus of around £45 million for the 30-year period, a sum of £40 million (£30 million at 1989 present values) would require to be obtained as public sector funding.

THE CURRENT POSITION

A programme of public awareness is being undertaken, not only about the present scheme, but also about LRT in general. The major route choices have just been made so that detailed design work can be undertaken in readiness for a bill to be deposited in parliament this November, and for a section 56 grant application to be submitted.

ACKNOWLEDGEMENTS

I would like to thank Roger Newman of Nottingham Development Enterprise and the staff of Nottinghamshire County Council for their help in the preparation of this feature.

◀An artist's impression of an NRT vehicle coming past Old Market Square, with the Council House in the background.

MANCHESTER
Making Tracks for Metrolink
by David Holt, Development Officer, LRTA

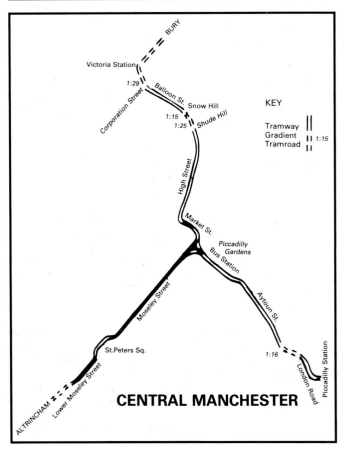

CENTRAL MANCHESTER

KEY

Tramway ‖
Gradient ‖ 1:15
Tramroad ‖

Seven years of hard work finally began to bear fruit in April 1990 when the UK's first new street tramway track in decades began to be laid for Manchester's Metrolink light rail network. This long-awaited development followed a year's preparatory work diverting or ducting various items of equipment which passed under the street alignments. It also followed a great deal of behind-the-scenes planning, consultation and decision-making backed up by local political support and professional commitment of the highest order.

The inception of tracklaying represents the start of the biggest construction project the city has seen in many a long year. It throws into even sharper perspective the demands made by Metrolink on those involved with it, for during the fallow years in this country the art of tram track construction and maintenance has been kept alive only at Blackpool and on museum premises (Crich et al). Today's engineers have applied their wider experience and resourcefulness to tackle street track installation.

CITY ALIGNMENT CRITERIA

The flexible nature of light rail invites planners to thread tracks tortuously through city centre streets. Maximum penetration with minimum property-take is the goal, the former to guarantee passenger appeal and the latter to minimise expense and parliamentary snags. The alignments are then defined for parliamentary purposes as tramways (on-street) and tramroads (off-street). Only the proposed track alignment is shown for tramways, while tramroads are marked on the parliamentary plans within fairly wide limits of deviation; the corridor within

which the permanent way engineer must work on the tramroads falls in practice well within these limits of deviation, which for compulsory purchase reasons have to spread around the boundaries of affected property adjacent to the alignment.

Basically, two separate criteria remain to be met when deciding the exact positioning, configuration and geometry of tram track. Conditions sometimes make it hard to fully reconcile them with each other.

The most obvious of these criteria is that the track must position not the wheels but the extremities of rail vehicle bodywork correctly at all times in relation to the built environment and to other traffic, including rail vehicles on adjacent tracks. Overhang on curves and the attitude of the door sills in relation to stopping-place platforms are just two of the factors to be taken into account. Minimum fixed structure clearances must be strictly observed, and agreement must be arrived at with highway authorities concerning proximity to footways and carriageways which in any case must be kept within prescribed limits.

The other criterium is not quite as obligatory as the first. Curve shapes initially engineered into street track will exert a permanent influence on passenger comfort levels, journey quality, tolerance of standee travel, wear and tear and so on. At any given speed, it is obvious that sharp curves inflict more dynamic disturbance on passengers than gentle curves. Furthermore, sharp curves which start or finish abruptly can inflict forces on standing passengers which are sudden enough to overcome their individual speed of reaction and strength.

These two criteria – basically 'miss buildings' and 'use large radii' – are nothing new, but in recent times the comfort factor has been thrown sharply into focus by the splendid provisions being made for the admittance of mobility-impaired passengers. Far from being confined to the removal of obstacles such as steps, improved access must also mean eliminating any unnecessary dynamic disturbance from LRT journeys. This in turn dictates gentle cornering and that is just what is being pursued in Manchester as far as conditions permit.

A CASE IN POINT: SNOW HILL

One location in particular provides a good example of the difficulties. To obtain a favourable alignment for the tramroad across Snow Hill, which lies between Balloon Street and High Street, Parliamentary powers were obtained by the PTE to acquire certain buildings so that they could be demolished to create a good corridor. However, because the buildings lay within a conservation area it was necessary to seek the City Council's consent to their demolition. This was granted for the majority of the buildings, but the Council could not be persuaded that numbers 17 and 19 Bradshaw Street had to be demolished in order to construct Metrolink.

No. 19 Bradshaw Street is the 'Castle and Falcon' public house. Local campaigners, especially CAMRA, put forward vigorous arguments for the hostelry's retention which, coupled with the City Council's own views, resulted in its remaining intact. As a consequence the alignment of Metrolink is now in a slightly different position from that originally conceived, having been moved laterally away from what remains of the 'Castle and Falcon', now owned and maintained by the PTE. This lateral shift has meant sharpening the curves from Balloon Street at one end and into High Street at the other. Thousands of future passengers will feel the effects in terms of marginally diminished journey quality.

Snow Hill also happens to be the location of a potential future stopping place. At the Victoria end of the site there must be a vertical curve merging with Balloon Street's rather steep down gradient. Because a straight, flat section of track the length of a coupled pair of LRVs is needed for the stopping-place, the vertical curve's location has had to be pushed to the far end of the proposed platforms and this in turn has meant sharpening its radius. Passengers will feel a correspondingly less gradual change of fore-and-aft forces as they ride over the sharpened "hump".

It must be emphasised that in both the lateral and vertical cases quoted, the additional dynamic disturbances and their effects on comfort levels, service speeds and wear and tear will be relatively mild. Nevertheless they are bound to be reflected in passengers' overall perception of journey quality, highlighting the level of care needed to arrive at the right compromise solutions when threading a light rail route through a mature and developing city centre.

As far as entering and leaving curves is concerned, this is being made as smooth as possible by building transitions into the great majority of curves having a radius of less than 80 m. This means that the radius changes gradually as the track turns into the curve rather than abruptly from straight to curved in no distance at all. Superelevation or cant, another way of improving cornering conditions for passengers, is also being applied where possible. This involves raising the outer rail on curves, lowering the inner or twisting the track about its centre line. The net effect is to reduce lateral cornering force on equipment and passengers; the application of cant is, however, constrained by the need not to tilt the highway surface unduly, disrupt surface drainage or exceed the twist tolerance of the articulated LRVs. Where possible up to 35 mm superelevation or cant is being built into tramroad and tramway curves. Again, transition portions ensure smooth entry to and exit from these sections.

THE CONTRACT

Metrolink is being brought into the world by means of a Design, Build, Operate and Maintain – or 'DBOM' – form of contract. This means that the GMA Consortium, selected by GMPTE/A last year, is carrying out all the detailed design, following the production of a reference specification by the PTE. John Mowlem & Co PLC, the consortium member responsible for all civil engineering (except for the Operations and Maintenance Centre and some BR work) have engaged W S Atkins Consultants as design consultants and Balfour Beatty Railway Engineering Ltd to install the rails themselves. The highway authority (Manchester City Council) is closely involved at all times as is GMPTE and GEC Alsthom Transportation Projects Ltd, the consortium member responsible for vehicles, power supplies, communications and so on.

TRACK DESIGN

Interfacing the tracks with the surface contortions of roads is one of the tasks to be undertaken. It is no simple matter to insert tracks, for example, flush across a road junction embodying complex changes of gradient – yet that is what is having to be done where the Metrolink tracks cross Shudehill and at other locations. Besides maintaining a safe and smooth path for road traffic there is also the LRVs' specified ability to tolerate compound track geometries to be taken into account. Drainage must be taken care of; the provisions which are being made for surface water disposal are comprehensive and sometimes far-reaching, and include the installation of rail drains where required.

As far as the positioning of the tracks is concerned, we have already seen how conflicting influences have to be reconciled. To achieve this reconciliation accurately, it follows that the design of city-centre track layouts and geometry has to be done with precision. The track itself then has to be installed with commensurate accuracy, not least so that passengers will enjoy the smoothest possible ride at the highest safe speed. After all, it is track configuration and geometry which ultimately constrain performance.

SLAB INSULATION

Close control of track alignment is therefore being exercised at all stages of the work. Generally, each track is treated as a separate structure. Lines are first set out far enough apart to include the trackside nests of ducts referred to later. Cuts are made in the road surface, followed by breaking-out and removal of the old material to form a channel approximately 0.5 metre deep. The bottom of the channel is levelled and compacted, then coated with a thin layer of well-tamped concrete as a working base ready for construction of the main 225 mm thick track slab.

The track structure is designed to be able to span a 2 metre

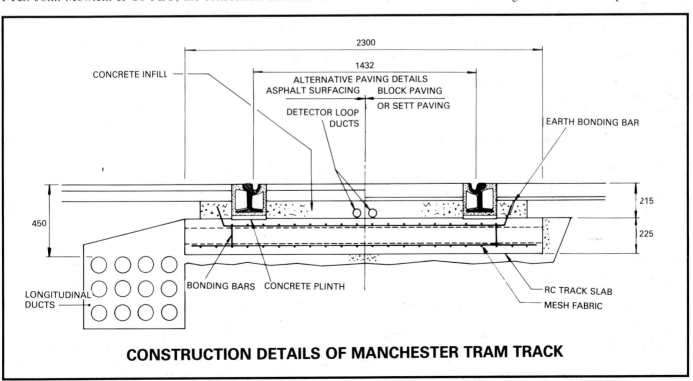

CONSTRUCTION DETAILS OF MANCHESTER TRAM TRACK

▲Aerial view showing the full length of initially-laid tram track. The white building at the bottom right is the 'Castle & Falcon' pub, with the Snow Hill alignment behind it. High Street stretches away to Market Street where the tracks turn left. *David Holt, courtesy CIS*

wide void resulting from such a cause as the fracture of a nearby water main. Two continuous layers of steel reinforcing mesh are placed along the formation between separating cast concrete pedestals and blocks. Further advantage is taken of the mesh by welding together adjacent sheets to form an electrically continuous cage underneath the track, connected to the traction return pole by frequent bonding cables. This is just one of the precautions being taken to minimise the quantity of return traction current that finds its way into underground pipes or cables where it could cause corrosion or electrical interference. At this stage any cross-ducts, such as those required for transponder loops, are put in place.

Formwork is next assembled along the sides and at the ends of the section, ready for the main concrete pour. Then special formwork assemblies are accurately positioned on top to form the shallow rebates or channels above which the rails will sit, together with kerb-like raised shoulders on either side of the line of each pair of rails. Considerably shortened sections of formwork are used to form horizontal and vertical curves; this ensures that the final level and position of the track, including any superelevation, will be accurately reflected in the shape of the concrete base slabs.

The bulk ready-mixed concrete is distributed by pumping it through a long flexible pipe. Vibrating pokers are used to eliminate voids as it settles into place, following which the top surface is shuffle-boarded and tamped level. After curing, the slab can be prepared for the rails themselves. To promote a high degree of accuracy, Mowlem's setting-out engineers fix small square plywood pads at frequent intervals to the surface of the concrete along the centre line of each track. Each pad bears information from which the exact position of the rails themselves can later be derived.

Meanwhile, work continues laying nests of up to 16 ducts

adjacent to each side of the alignment. These ducts will be used for traction power, earth bonding, communications, video and signalling. Spare capacity will be available for renting-off. Draw pits are being installed, normally placed outside the swept path for reasons of access, every 50 metres.

The surfaces of any intersecting roads are temporarily reinstated over the top of the prepared concrete base using asphalt so that traffic can continue to flow normally. Tracklaying across roads is generally done in two halves, with pre-cast concrete slabs being installed at particularly busy intersections during weekend occupations. Keeping the city moving at all times is an important and often difficult part of the work; the city's computerised Urban Traffic Control system is being used to good advantage and care is taken to keep the public well informed. That so much has been accomplished with so few problems so far must go on record as a great tribute to the PTE, the City Engineers, the Contractors and not least to the people of Manchester who have shown such exemplary forbearance.

WHEEL AND RAIL SELECTION

Wheel/rail design is the responsibility of the Consortium and is to a great extent dictated by the nature of the project. Metrolink trams will have to run at 80 km/h on railway track as well as entering the street. Street compatibility means that the back-to-back dimension cannot be reduced sufficiently to engage existing railway check and wing rails. A solution which was developed for LRV operation over railway tracks in Karlsruhe (Germany) will be adopted here. The wheelsets will have a reduced back-to-back dimension at a slightly smaller diameter than the tread. This will provide an inside wheel 'rim' which can engage specially-raised check and wing rails at points and crossings on railway track, but which will run clear of any street trackwork. By this means off-street inter-running with heavy railway wheelsets can be maintained where it is required.

Another feature of the existing railway track which influences choice of wheel profile is the 1 in 20 inward rail inclination already featured by the railway tracks to Bury and Altrincham over which Metrolink LRVs will have to run at speeds of up to 80 km/h. Because of the high proportion of this type of running, Metrolink's wheel tread coning will be made compatible with the ex-railway rails' inwardly-inclined running surfaces, the profile adopted being in fact a modified version of the BR standard P8 wheel profile.

Unlike railway rails, grooved tramway rails are generally laid upright with no inward inclination. Part of the reason for this is the extreme difficulty of carrying rail inclination round a sharp corner while maintaining gauge and without building-in unwanted stresses – just try bending an ordinary desk ruler and inclining it inwards throughout its length at the same time. So that the grooved rail running surface will, from the day operation commences, be presented to the wheels (and to the track brake pole faces) at the same angle as the ex-railway rails with which the coning is compatible, it is proposed to grind the running surfaces of the grooved rails just sufficiently to apply the requisite inclination.

The type of track surfacing to be adopted has not yet, owing to the DBOM form of contract, been decided for all locations. It is, however, already known that none of the city-centre trackwork is likely to be left open, even where it runs off-street. Not surprisingly, then, grooved rail has been chosen for use throughout the city-centre, Ri59 being the section selected. It weighs in at 59 kg/m and has a groove width of 42 mm; the first three hundred 18 m lengths of it, rolled in Luxembourg, were delivered on 23rd July. Its wide, deep flangeway will, as well as accommodating the Metrolink flanges, eliminate any need to use a different rail section on curves. Widening the gauge on curves will also be unnecessary.

RAIL ENCAPSULATION

Once the continuous concrete bases have been installed by Mowlem's 30-strong site workforce, Balfour Beatty Railway Engineering can follow on with rail installation. The first section to be tackled by the 15-strong BB team was the straight, level portion of off-street alignment passing through the site of the projected station at Snow Hill.

▼ Looking from the site of the High Street profiled platform, the depression of the platform track (nearest to the camera) can be clearly seen. In the background a Thermit weld is being made at a rail joint; flames and smoke billow from the crucible after ignition of the Thermit mixture. *David Holt*

Many different methods have over the years been used to fix grooved rails in position and interface road material to them. One elusive goal has always been the elimination of corrugations, which have in the past frustrated all manner of counter-measures. Unlike road-only vehicles, trams are unfairly expected to be seen and not heard and this demands special and expensive track construction techniques – even though Manchester's LRVs will be fitted with Bochum resilient wheels. Other important permanent way objectives are the maintenance of gauge, the prevention of water ingress and the protection of the substructure against rail movement on its surface.

Metrolink's grooved rails are being encapsulated in a polyurethane based material which fixes them firmly in place so that in effect each rail is completely suspended in a flexible grout. No permanent tie-bars are at present being fitted, although temporary tie-bars are being used during assembly and positioning of curves. These will facilitate gauge adjustment and help support the rails during the encapsulation process. There are no mechanical rail anchorages.

SikaRail KC330, the load-bearing resilient grout being used in Manchester, was used by Balfour Beatty in Tuen Mun (Hong Kong) and before that by many undertakings including Frankfurt as long ago as 1974. Sika also produce a family of complimentary products for use with KC330 a new softer grade of which, designated KC330/UK, was developed for Manchester at the request of W S Atkins, Mowlem's consulting engineers. An extensive programme of compliance testing was carried out to convince the consultants that the product met their stringent requirements. Balfour Beatty gained further confidence by installing a short length of encapsulated track in their works for their own tests.

By absorbing vibrations the SikaRail resilient liquid-applied grout/ fixation system results in smoother and quieter running, while its excellent electrical insulating properties assist with confining return traction current to the rails themselves. There appears to be every reason to have confidence in this form of track construction, which should overcome many of the maintenance problems historically associated with street track. If at some time in the future the grout has to be removed for any track maintenance operation, such as repair welding, it can be cut out by means of a high-pressure water lance.

Preparation for rail-laying starts with needle-gunning the concrete base channels so as to expose the aggregate and provide a good key. Then a screed is laid in each channel, consist

▼ A few seconds later and the fusible plug has automatically tapped the Thermit reaction crucible; white-hot molten steel can be seen filling up the mould-encased joint. *David Holt*

ing of Sika Latex, cement and fine aggregate. This initial screed does not have resilient properties, its actual purpose being to accurately make up the concrete base under the rails. Balfour Beatty Railway Engineering, Mowlem's sub-contractor, now move in to undertake track installation. Before encapsulation the bases of the rails are thoroughly prepared underneath and given an initial coat of primer. They are also welded into one continuous length.

RAIL BENDING

During the encapsulation processes, everything must be kept dry. Protection against Manchester's occasional shower is obtained by means of long, arched awnings into which heated air can be blown. These awnings have to be able to accommodate themselves to the bends which proliferate on the city-centre alignments and which necessitate a considerable amount of arduous rail-bending. Grooved tramway rail is much more rigid than railway rail and it has to be bent to far smaller radii – as sharp as 25 m radius on Metrolink. Because of the magnitude of the rail-bending work, Balfour Beatty have brought onto site an impressive rail-bending machine manufactured by Geismar, a French firm having its British base in Northampton. A similar machine was used by Balfour Beatty in Tuen Mun.

Not all of the horizontal bending is being done with the large machine; for some of the work a Geismar B60 'jim crow' is being used. This more traditional type of rail bender acts against opposite sides of the rail via three pads shaped to fit the rail to ensure that the bending force is applied squarely and that no twist is put into the rail. The middle pad supports the rail while the outermost pair are pushed against it by hydraulic rams, putting a bend into the rail in the vicinity of the centremost pad. When this is done at short intervals, the rail assumes a smoothly curved shape. The machine is shifted along and pumped manually.

The much more substantial Geismar VO406 rail-bending machine is equipped with six rollers arranged on its top surface in three pairs like the spots on an elongated die. The rollers are interchangeable to fit different types of rail. As tram rail is asymmetric the rollers are handed and must be swapped over for bending opposite rails. Of the six rollers, the first two pairs grip the rail and drive it slowly forward. The third pair, which do the actual bending, are mounted on a carriage which can be traversed laterally by a hydraulic ram to exert the bending force. The whole machine is controlled by one man using fingertip controls and is self-contained with its own petrol engine. It is set up for bending sessions within the alignment itself. The first time it was used was on High Street to bend the rails which curve across Shudehill from Snow Hill.

The rail to be bent is raised to the working level of the machine by placing it on roller-topped trestles which enable it to slide easily to and fro. Chalk marks are made at regular intervals. The rail is then gripped by the first two pairs of rollers and driven forward until it is engaged by the third pair, which are then traversed until the desired sideways force (up to 40 tonnes) is being applied. As the rail moves majestically forward between the rollers it assumes a smooth curved shape which is checked for radius, using a chord-and-versine formula, as soon as the length between two chalk marks has been bent. If the radius is not right, the section is simply passed back through the machine for fine adjustment. Applying the bend in this way is fast and it ensures accurate and continuous control as well as facilitating the production of transition curves. 300 or so millimetres at the end of each rail cannot be bent by this or any other known method because there is nothing beyond it to grip. These unbent ends are cut off using a Geismar MTX302 abrasive disc rail cutter.

The newly-bent rail emerges from the machine onto another series of roller-topped trestles from where it is lowered onto rollers resting on the formation; all rail hoisting and lowering is done using gantries with traversing chain-blocks. The absence of any drillings in the webs of the rails makes handling them rather difficult, there being nowhere to insert lifting gear; slings are used instead. Once on the rollers, the rail can be manhandled into its final position for welding to its neighbours. Any final adjustments to radius are made on the ground by hydraulic 'jim crow'.

THERMIT WELDING

Welding of the rail joints is done by Thermit-trained Balfour Beatty men. The aluminothermic process, which uses a mixture of finely divided iron oxide, metallic aluminium powder and alloying agents, is spectacular, sublimely elegant and much appreciated by passers-by. A barbeque umbrella provides practical and rather picturesque shelter during rain – not for the passers by or for the operatives, but for the joint and equipment during setting-up. The rails are first clamped firmly in line by means of a jig, leaving a gap between the cleaned ends of the rails. Preformed sand moulds are clamped about the joint and the reaction crucible lined up carefully above before being swivelled aside while the whole assembly, including rail ends, is preheated to 600–700°C by oxy-propane torch.

The crucible, already charged with the right quantity of active mixture, is then swung back over the joint and the reaction started by inserting a Thermit igniter through its open neck. Flames and smoke issue from the crucible which in a few seconds is full of molten steel at a temperature of up to 3000°C which, tapped automatically by fusible plug, flows white-hot down into the joint. Two or three minutes afterwards, the moulds are broken away and excess metal is trimmed from the rail head by air chisel while still red hot. The moulds are removed and later the top part of the rail is ground smooth so as to form a true running surface. One pair of operatives can complete a Thermit joint in less than 30 minutes.

Once in position and continuously welded the rails are finally set up ready for encapsulation. The combined rail-gauge and spirit level is fitted at its centre with a plumb-bob which is used to accurately line up the track from the plywood pad datum points. Conventional surveying techniques are used to confirm accuracy. It is at this stage that any superelevation is finally set up. When they have been positioned accurately the rails are temporarily secured by locating spikes and by sleeper-like steel jigs pandrol-clipped to their bases. Packing pieces, later replaced with poured polymer pads, maintain the rails at the correct height. The upper flanks of the rails are prepared and primed followed by fixing of rectangular PVC ballast tubes into the webs using a thixotropic grade of SikaRail KC330. The ballast tubes fully occupy the spaces either side of the web between rail base and head and will later be filled with mortar to increase the effective mass of the rails, helping to damp out vibrations.

SikaRail primer is applied to the rail-bases, the surface of the screed and the outer flanks of the ballast tubes by roller, again in absolutely dry awning-covered conditions. Plywood-supported PVC shuttering is next fitted at either side of each rail. All is now ready for the grouting operation. KC330/UK is a two pack product, the two parts being mixed together just before application. During the initial pour, the polymer flows into place under and around the bases of the rails, where it will cure to form a tough 25 mm thick resilient anchorage. Further grout, bulked up with sand, is mixed and poured to form a 20 mm thick 'wall' up either side of each rail, most of which adheres to the primed ballast tube flanks rather than to the rails themselves. At this stage, the grout is only carried half way up the rail head. The shuttering is afterwards removed.

SURFACING

Details of surface finish will vary according to location. Where hot rolled asphalt is used, it will be applied up to rail-top level, allowed to cool then milled out either side of the rail head down to the level of the polymer. After suitable treatment of the rail faces the resulting channels will be filled to surface level with SikaRail grout. This sequence is being adopted to ensure that a permanent waterproof bond is obtained between grout and road surface.

As the work progresses, discussions continue between Mowlem, W S Atkins, the City Engineer and the PTE to select suitable surface finishes according to the circumstances prevailing in each location. At the top end of Market Street, for instance, the tracks pass through a pedestrianised area where there will be a profiled station platform. Many conflicting requirements have to be reconciled and the right compromise solution identified. Grey precast concrete block surfacing is being considered for the Market Street tramway, the tracks of which are separated here by a unidirectional busway which will be finished with asphalt. The footways, slightly reduced in width, will be surfaced by re-using the existing pale yellow slabs. The footway/tramway margin will be signified by grey kerbstones having shallow-angled tops sloping down from footway level, together with a very shallow final drop to the slightly lower tramway level. Such a profile will give visually-handicapped pedestrians and their guide dogs distinctive orientation clues as well as allowing wheelchairs and baby buggies to roll easily across. The busway/ tramway interface will be distinguished by kerbstones chamfered to permit occasional mounting by emergency vehicles.

When grouting is complete, ready-mixed concrete is poured in on top of the already-cast base slab until it has filled the spaces between the rails themselves and between the rails and the cast concrete shoulders either side of each track. Carried up to approximately half the height of the rails, this additional concrete both supports and permanently locates them and at the same time forms a solid base for the surfacing treatment.

TRAM TRACK: THE NON-USER BENEFITS.

The Metrolink tracks and their reinforced concrete bases will enhance the streets they pass through. The well-finished alignments will provide an immensely strong, permanently smooth surface for buses, including competing buses, other heavy vehicles and cars. Damage done by heavy-axled road-only vehicles to adjacent buildings, sewers and other services should be substantially reduced if not eliminated along these streets thanks to Metrolink. These significant non-user benefits deserve to be recognised, quantified and credited to light rail.

POINTWORK

Beyond Market Street will lie the triangular junction forming the hub of Metrolink. Edgar Allen Engineering, based in Sheffield, have been accustomed since the turn of the century to supplying complete tramway junction layouts cast throughout in manganese steel – the firm is currently fulfilling a big export order for the Toronto Transit Commission. For Manchester's triangular junction, Edgar Allen will be supplying only the manganese steel diamond and turnout crossings; the 1 in 20 head inclination referred to earlier is being designed into the castings. The point switches themselves are to be in carbon rail steel, supplied by Balfour Beatty Railway Engineering Ltd., switches and diamonds will be brought together on site. Point motors will be by Hanning & Kahl. The only crossover in the city centre will be located on Aytoun Street, for turning cars back short of Piccadilly station when required.

FOOTNOTE

As the work progresses problems are being resolved in the light of experience. The procedures described here were used for track installed during 1990 and have been modified since so that all concrete is cast before installation of the rails into the channels which are created. The shape of the ballast tubes has also been modified.

ACKNOWLEDGEMENTS

The author gratefully acknowledges help given with the preparation of this article by:
GMPTE, Manchester City Engineer, John Mowlem & Co PLC, W S Atkins Consultants, GEC Alsthom Transportation Projects Ltd, Balfour Beatty Railway Engineering Ltd, Sika Ltd, Geismar Ltd, Thermit Welding (GB) Ltd, Edgar Allen Engineering Ltd.

The Geismar V0406 rail bending machine in use on High Street. The left hand pair of rollers have been traversed sideways to apply the bending force while the rail is driven through from right to left by the other four rollers. The machine's engine can be seen in front of the operator.   *David Holt*

METROLINK UPDATE by David Holt

Metrolink is scheduled to go into public service on Monday 23rd September with 14 LRVs running between Manchester Victoria and Bury. From July, trains from Bury will run only as far as Crumpsall; passengers for Woodlands Road and Victoria will continue their journeys by substitute bus. This is to allow time for initial Metrolink driver training using as a base the new depot and works being constructed at the Queens Road headquarters, and to permit connection of the Bury line track with the new street track where it penetrates Victoria station.

Five weeks before 23rd September, the existing Bury electric trains will cease running to allow time for removal of the third rail, registration of the new overhead wire, accurate alignment of the track relative to platform faces and other work. Ongoing BR rolling stock shortages mean that no substitute diesel units will be available during the five week changeover period and for this reason a replacement bus service will have to be operated throughout the full length of the line.

Some six weeks after the Bury–Victoria reopening, around the end of October or the beginning of November 1991, the Bury service will be extended through the streets to Piccadilly BR station; street track construction is proceeding steadily and is covered in a separate article. LRVs will also be able to operate in November 1991 to G-MEX where a major light rail exhibition and conference is scheduled to take place. A review

of the proposed alignment through St Peter's Square is being undertaken. Construction of the ramped viaduct which will take the tracks up from Lower Mosley Street to the level of the G-MEX (ex-Central station) approach viaducts is well in hand.

The BR track layout at Altrincham is scheduled for remodelling in readiness for Metrolink during the first two weeks of July 1991. Existing train services between Altrincham and Manchester are scheduled to cease on 24th December 1991 so that conversion work can be undertaken; there will be replacement buses between Deansgate station and Altrincham. Reopening of the Altrincham line as a Metrolink service through the city centre to Piccadilly BR is scheduled for Monday 27th January 1992.

Work has already started in Italy constructing the fleet of 26 LRVs which will be equipped by Firema with electrical and control gear supplied by GEC Alsthom before being brought as complete vehicles by road to this country, the first arrival being expected at Queens Road on 23rd May 1991. The mockup bodyshell has had its livery modified to reflect the operating company's corporate image and has also undergone detailed passenger equipment changes.

On the Bury line, work is being carried out to bring station access facilities up to the high standards set for Metrolink. For the most part this involves construction of easily-graded ramps connecting platforms with nearby streets although in one or two cases lifts will have to be provided. Similar work on the Altrincham line will follow. Other work at existing stations includes creating LRV-sized holes through walls at Victoria and Piccadilly, preparation of an LRT alignment inside Victoria station and work in Piccadilly Undercroft to transform it into a surface-level 'underground' LRT station.

Plans to increase the future size of the light rail network are being vigorously pursued in the face of great uncertainty over the availability of public and private funding. In a comprehensive study the PTE has been looking at the possibilities for converting the Oldham and Rochdale line to LRT operation, including unsegregated penetration of both town centres. Further progress with the planned extension into Trafford Park awaits a Government decision on the major new shopping centre planned for Dumplington, the line's projected terminus. The LRT underpass under construction at Cornbrook incorporates facilities for a future junction serving both the Trafford Park line and projected Salford Quays line as well as a possible future station acting as an interchange point as well as providing good access to redeveloping areas nearby.

◄High Street looking from Church Street towards Market Street corner. A profiled platform will be located in the space visible to the left of the tracks here.   *David Holt*

GATHERING MOMENTUM
Low-Floor LRV Progress
by Michael Taplin

INTRODUCTION

Light Rail Review 1 described how the planner's goal of level access to light rail vehicles was being achieved in two ways. Firstly using traditional high-floor cars, but with every stop equipped with a high platform to match (as in Calgary, Utrecht and Istanbul for instance). Secondly with new car designs featuring novel engineering to achieve a low floor over part or all of the car length.

On established systems the first option is scarcely feasible, given the construction work that would be required at each stop (and would be impossible at most street stops), but operators are generally raising the height of loading islands or platforms at segregated stops where this is possible. This permits a minimum first step in to the car, and perhaps level access if an appropriate design of low-floor car follows.

Even on new systems the high platform option is difficult to achieve without constraining the inherent flexibility of light rail, and perhaps upsetting city planners who see high platforms and the resulting station as an unwelcome and intrusive barrier. The area required is increased significantly by the ramps that have to be provided to permit easy wheelchair and pram access to the platform.

Social and political pressures are now firmly behind giving the mobility impaired easy access to regular public transport services, and although some progress has been made with low-floor buses (particularly in Germany), the problem is more easily resolved with the rail-guided vehicle, whose position in relation to a fixed platform can be aligned precisely. Thus where Geneva and Grenoble showed the way, more and more are seeking to follow.

▶ Duewag's latest design for Kassel represents a half-way transition to the full low-floor design, with EEF trucks supporting the centre section and three of the five doors featuring direct access to the low-floor section. *Duewag AG*

▶▼ The Vevey design developed for Geneva, with a small-wheel carrying bogie, does not permit level access, but the two low steps make life easier for those who would have difficulty climbing normal tram or bus steps. *M. R. Taplin*

▼ Boarding and alighting of large numbers of passengers from Geneva's two-car sets is speeded thanks to the low-floor design. *M. R. Taplin*

CARS WITH SHORT LOW-FLOOR SECTION

There are broadly three types of low-floor tram. Firstly cars with a low-floor section occupying less than 20% of the car length. This is the easiest solution, generally achieved by a low-floor centre section in a three-section car. Conventional bogies can be retained since the low-floor area is wholly between the bogies. Examples can be seen in Amsterdam, Basel, Freiburg-im-Breisgau and Würzburg, with Mannheim and Nantes joining the group in 1991. Basel, Mannheim and Nantes are rebuilds of earlier high-floor two-section trams.

The low-floor area is rather small (3.2 x 1.7 m in the LHB car for Würzburg), with access through only one door, and it breaks up the passage through the car from one high-floor section to another. Nevertheless the simple engineering solution permits the lowest of low floors to be achieved; 270 mm above rail height on the Duewag car for Freiburg, so that every stop could be equipped for level access with few problems. A few days in Basel will show two different primary uses for the low-floor centre section. On weekdays it becomes a kind of social club for mothers with children in pushchairs and prams, who are no longer housebound because they have no individual daytime transport. On Sundays the cyclists take over, carrying their bikes out to the edge of the suburbs for country rides.

CARS WITH MEDIUM LOW-FLOOR SECTION

The second group of cars is those with a low-floor occupying between 50 and 80% of the car length. Again the engineering solution is well-proven. Conventional motor bogies at the outer ends; small wheel or axleless truck at the central articu-

▲ The latest development of the Vevey design with its small-wheel carrying bogies is the eight-axle car for Bern delivered in 1990.
M.R. Taplin

◄ The biggest fleet of low-floor cars so far is the 54 delivered by Fiat to Torino. The short central section rests on an unmotored truck with independent wheels. *Fiat*

▼ SOCIMI's low-floor design for Roma follows on from Fiat's similar car for Torino, with a high floor over the motor bogies, and a short centre section supported by an independent wheel bogie. *SOCIMI*

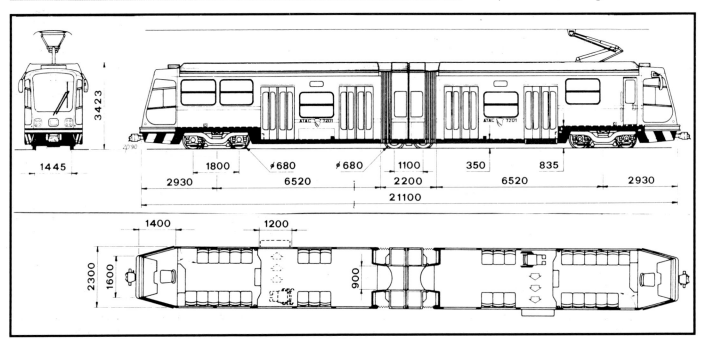

lation(s) permitting a gangway at the low-floor height throughout the car. Vevey devised the solution using small-wheel bogies, with deliveries to Geneva and Bern to be followed in 1991 by St Etienne. Grenoble led the way with the other solution, closely followed by the Italians where there are large batches of trams in Roma and Torino, and a prototype in Milano. The Grenoble design has been adopted for the Paris suburban route between St Denis and Bobigny now under construction, and will probably be bought by Reims and Rouen as well. Strasbourg wants a low-floor throughout the car, which is probably causing the GEC-Alsthom engineers to work overtime.

The German equivalent arrived in Kassel in November 1990. This three-section design will be the first to feature the EEF self-steering individual wheel truck developed by Duewag, albeit in non-motorised form, supporting the centre section. Bochum-Gelsenkirchen has ordered a two-section version. This will have the latest Siemens electrical equipment, with ac drives and gate-turn-off pulse-width-modulated thyristor inverters. The small three-phase ac motors permit the floor height over the motor bogies to be as low as 590 mm, so there will be only one step to the 340 mm low-floor section.

Cautious engineers see this group of cars as the low-risk low-floor option, offering something for everyone. Although there are steps within the car to reach the high-floor section, operating experience shows that these are not a problem in passenger service. Indeed longer distance passengers can tuck themselves away at the ends of the cars on the high-floor seats, away from the bustle of boarding and alighting short-distance passengers. One problem that does start to become apparent on these designs is the protrusion of the wheel arches into the passenger compartment, requiring some seats to be placed on pedestals above the floor height, making them less accessible to some passengers.

Other designs of this type seem likely to emerge; work has started in the design office of CKD Tatra in Praha, and with a large new factory coming on stream capable of producing over 500 articulated trams each year, the Czech firm should be able to offer economies of scale. Systems with steep gradients requiring adhesion in excess of 65% need cars with all axles motored, so an articulated tram would require centre motored bogie(s). Sheffield had to solve this problem whilst retaining a low-floor design, and has opted for a solution offered by Siemens/ Duewag. An eight-axle car with four motor bogies and a low-floor between the bogies in the outer sections, with the doors also located in this area. This means four sets of steps within the car, but is a low-risk technical solution.

CARS WITH A LOW FLOOR THROUGHOUT

The third type of low-floor car has the low-floor throughout the length of the passenger area. When Light Rail Review 1 was published the only design to have achieved this with a working prototype was the SOCIMI single car on trial in Milano. Little has been heard of the success of this car with eight individual wheels each driven by its own motor, and the articulated version has still to appear.

First to produce a working prototype of an articulated tram with low-floor throughout was MAN, with the design for Bremen heralded in Light Rail Review 1. Originally designed to reduce weight and costs by producing a three-section car mounted on three bogies rather than four, when interest in low floor trams became evident the new bogie was developed further to permit this feature to be added.

The bogie design is an elegant technical solution permitting a 350 mm gangway through a motored bogie. A body-mounted motor drives through a primary cardan shaft to a primary gearbox located externally to one end of the bogie frame, and integral with the secondary gearbox driving the adjoining wheel. This gearbox drives the other wheel by a transverse low-level cross shaft which is mounted outside the bogie frame, and whose other end drives the secondary gearbox for the

remote wheel. Kiepe Elektrik provide direct pulse inverter a.c. drive. This car has been running in public service for some months, three more are about to be delivered to München and 11 of a metre-gauge version have been ordered by Augsburg. No doubt the operators will be closely monitoring maintenance costs and ride quality

Hard on the heels of the MAN prototype came that designed and built by BN in Belgium. This long-established tramcar builder, now owned by the Canadian Bombardier group, built most of Western Europe's PCC cars, but recently showed more interest in developing its GLT guided bus system. However the prospect of a revival in Belgian tramcar orders saw the body shell for the third GLT transformed into a prototype low-floor tram.

This is mounted on independent wheel, articulated, maximum-traction, radial bogies (developed from those designed for the TAU automated mini-metro) with the 40 kW asynchronous squirrel-cage motors integrated with the powered wheels. The design is modular and can be offered with two to four body sections varying in length from 18 to 42 m, single or double-ended. The through floor height is 350 mm, with a minimum 800 mm gangway through the bogie. The only seats that require mounting on 200 mm podia are the two positioned back-to-back over the driving wheels of each bogie. The standard-gauge articulated bogie permits a minimum curve radius of 25 m in passenger service. Each bogie weights 2.5 t and a three section car on four bogies would weigh 37 t. In this version the bogies support the centre section rather than being mounted under the articulation.

This striking design, baptised LRV2000, has now run trials in Brussels (who have invited international tenders for 50 low-floor cars). These had to be carried out at night, because the 2.5 m body width of the prototype (dictated by the use of the GLT bus body) makes the car out-of-gauge in the city where the maximum tram width is 2.2 m. A visit to Wien (Vienna) may have followed, for the Austrian car builder Rotax is also in the Bombardier group, and Wien is looking for some low-floor cars for its Stadtbahn line. With its small guiding wheels and no less than 11 swivel points in each bogie, operators are probably going to want to see a considerable test mileage accumulated with this design before committing themselves.

The Italian firm of Breda sprung a surprise in May 1990 when they unveiled their VLC 001 with a working prototype carrying the Pininfarina styling cachet. Designed around the three principles of flexibility, accessibility and lightness, this three-section articulated car has two motor bogies at the outer ends with electrical equipment mounted in cabinets above these bogies, two individual wheel self-steering trucks supporting the articulation and a continuous floor level of 350 mm through the passenger area. The light alloy body is bolted rather than welded and wide use is made of composite materials to keep weight to a minimum while retaining maximum strength through bonding. It is a completely modular design with driving cab, motor bogie plus electrical equipment, passenger compartment, and articulation plus trailing truck capable of being assembled in various combinations. Electrical equipment is of the inverter GTO type, with three-phase asynchronous traction motors. The transverse motors transmit power through a differential to one cardan shaft for each axle. The prototype weighs 22 t, a remarkable achievment.

Mounting electrical equipment within the car body was the solution chosen initially by Vevey with its Geneva design, but its second generation car for Bern had the equipment in roof cabinets, as do the other designs described above. The Breda car will offer ease of accessibility, without resorting to roof gantries, at the expense of 2.8 m of additional length. The prototype is to run trials in Rome.

Due to appear in Spring 1991 is the long-awaited 100% low-floor design sponsored by the German operators' association VÖV. Developed by a consortium of rolling stock and electrical companies with a DM 45 million budget over a period of

▲ MAN won the race to produce the first tram with a low floor throughout, and their novel design is seen in service in Bremen on 19th September 1990.   *Peter Fox*

◄ This interior view of the MAN car demonstrates the residual problem of certain seats having to be mounted on podia.   *Peter Fox*

▼ More radical is Breda's modular design with a low floor throughout the passenger compartment and equipment modules above the motored bogies. *Breda*

▲ BN's prototype car with low floor throughout was built using the body shells of a guided bus design.　　　*BN*

▶ Test runs of the BN prototype had to take place at night in Brussels since the width of the car is outside the tramway loading gauge.　　　*AMUTRA*

▼▶ This drawing shows the design of the BN BA2000 bogie for low-floor trams.　*BN*

▼ A side view of the BN bogie, showing how two pairs of seats have to be mounted above the low-floor level.　　　*BN*

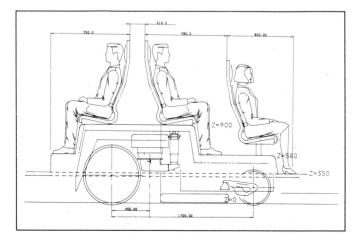

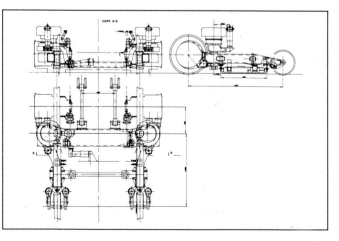

five years, the careful research and long trials of key components suggest a design that will offer maximum reliability. This is another modular design, with prototypes due to appear as a steel-bodied, two-section, double-ended car; an aluminium-bodied, two-section, single-ended car; and a steel-bodied three-section single-ended car.

Key to the design is a self-steering, individual wheel, EEF (Einzelrad-Einzel-Fahrwerk) truck developed by Prof. Dr. F. Frederich of Aachen Technical University from a back-to-basics study of wheel/rail interaction, in both motorised and trailing forms. Advantages are low construction height, permitting a 350 mm floor height through the wheel centres with no reduction in gangway width, low weight and small volume, reduced noise and maintenance, standard wheel size for the entire car and equal wheel wear. The truck, built by BSI, is equipped with one AEG 60 kW motor driving each wheel through an integrated drive, controlled by the Siemens SIBAS 16 control system and water-cooled ABB inverters. Hydraulic braking is supplied by Hanning & Kahl. Because, unlike a bogie, there is no primary suspension, the EEF requires special SAB resilient wheels with conical rubber rings pressed into a V-shaped slot between hub and wheel rim.

The truck works by the interaction of the near-convex wheel profile with any railhead profile to give a stable equilibrium, swivelling the wheel into its ideal tangential position. A primary condition for this is the arrangement of the swivelling pivot on the outer side of the wheel gauge (negative swivelling radius, as opposed to the zero or positive swivelling radii used for experiments with radial trucks in the 1930s). Both wheels control each other by a short steering rod linked to the swivels by inside steering levers. As the two individual wheels swivel around their vertical axes (located outside the wheels), the truck itself remains in line with the body centreline, unlike a conventional bogie.

The VÖV car is expected to attract 300-400 orders within a short space of time, since many German cities have postponed rolling stock replacement pending completion of the development programme, while many tramways in the former East Germany (DDR) will be looking for new rolling stock. The prototypes will run in Bonn, Düsseldorf, Ludwigshafen, Mannheim and München.

The final entirely low-floor car design being built is a batch of trailers for Geneva by Vevey. Using the small wheel bogies developed as trailing bogies for the Geneva and Bern articulated trams, a four-axle trailer with a through 350 mm floor height is being built to provide extra capacity on a new route to the main railway station.

Thus it can be seen that much effort is being expended and development funding committed to find the ideal solution to the low-floor problem. With any wheeled vehicle (including buses) there will always be a trade-off between the minimum floor height and the number of sets that have to be mounted on podia, thus reducing the effective minimum floor height. The highest feasible platform at each stop will reduce the need for such a trade-off, and designers of new systems would do well to remember this. However the tramcar manufacturers will be trying to meet the market for about 300 new trams each year from the existing operators, who do not have so much freedom of choice.

COMPARATIVE SPECIFICATIONS OF LOW-FLOOR LRVs

	Duewag Kassel	MAN Bremen	BN LRV2000	Breda VLC001	VöV/ EEF
Overall length (m)	28.75	26.50	30.06	22.00	26.69
Body width (m)	2.30	2.30	2.40	2.50	2.30
Body height (m)	3.23	3.30	3.425	2.95	3.24
Truck centre separation (m)	7.65+6.20	8.50	7.92+7.32	6.70+6.00	7.30+5.80
Overhang (m)	2.10	2.95	3.45	1.30	3.50
Bogie wheelbase (m)	1.80	1.85	1.70	1.40	–
Minimum curve radius (m)	18	?	25*	18	18
Wheel diameter (new) (mm)	560	680	650	680	560
Floor height (mm)	350+720	300–350	350	350	290–350
Unladen weight (t)	29	26.8	37	22	24
Motors (kW)	2 x 180	3 x 84	8 x 40	2 x 205	3 x 60
Seats/standing	80/105	67/103	62/108	36/141	74/79

* 18 m with double-articulated bogie

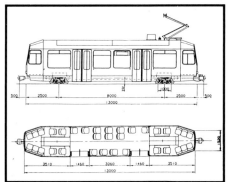

▲ Vevey's design for a Geneva trailer with small-wheel bogies to permit a low floor throughout. The pantograph will collect power for the auxiliaries. *Vevey*

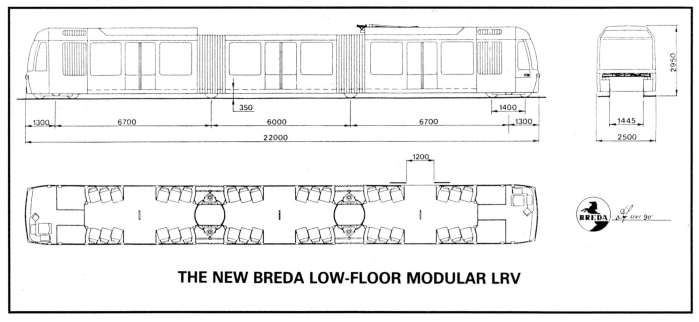

THE NEW BREDA LOW-FLOOR MODULAR LRV

CANADA
Toronto's new Light Rail Line
by E.A. Wickson

Toronto, Canada, is admired throughout America for the quality of its transit service, which has been under municipal control since 1921. Once the operator of a large fleet of PCC trams (744 cars), the Toronto Transit Commission concentrated on metro construction in the 1950s and 1960s, closing many tram routes in the process. At one stage the tramway system was slated for complete abandonment, but increasing citizens' protests at this policy led to a 1972 decision to retain tramways indefinitely on the seven surviving routes. 196 new trams were delivered in 1978–82, followed by 52 articulated cars in 1988–90. A number of PCC cars remain in traffic, with some recently rebuilt for a further decade of service.

The decision to retain trams led to proposals to build new routes, on the lower part of Spadina Ave (connecting with the metro along the northern part), from the metro terminus at Kennedy to the new suburban centre at Scarborough, and along the harbourfront to serve an area isolated by railway yards and an expressway, but with developing office, residential and recreational facilities. The Spadina line became embroiled in controversy that has only just been resolved (with a decision to proceed taken on 16 August 1990), the Kennedy–Scarborough line was built using the automated mini-metro developed by the Urban Transit Development Corporation,

which left the Harbourfront line to taken the honours of Toronto's first new tramway for 60 years when it was opened on 22nd June 1990.

The purpose of the Harbourfront Light Rail transit (a title selected to indicate a design philosophy upgraded from that of the traditional streetcar or tramway) is to reunite Toronto's central waterfront with the city's downtown core. The 2.1 km line cost CD$ 59.3 million, but that includes a 600 m subway to provide interchange with the metro at Union Station and position the line in the median strip of Queens Quay without interference from motor traffic. The western terminus is at the south end of Spadina Avenue, where service tracks provide access to the existing tramway system for depot journeys (but will be used by the Spadina line mentioned above). Along Queens Quay the line is on a reservation raised 120 mm above road level.

Construction of the line started in October 1987, after considerable debate concerning the alleged "barrier" effect of the

▼ Most of the Toronto system is traditional street tramway. This Canadian Light Rail Vehicle westbound on Queen St stops other traffic to permit passengers to board and light from the kerb.

E.A. Wickson

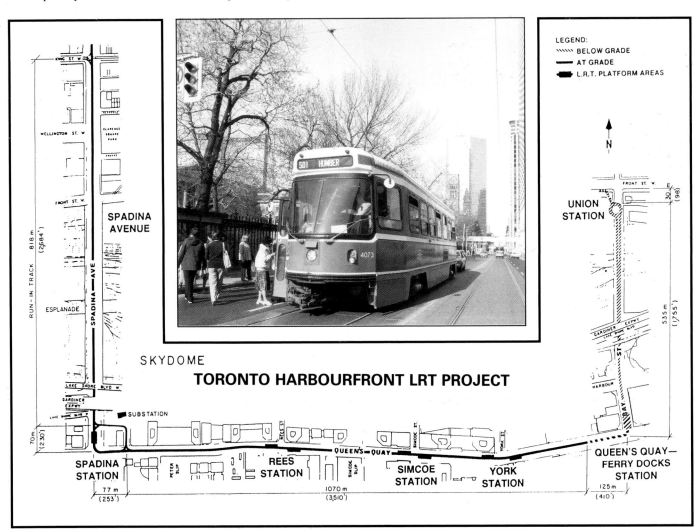

TORONTO HARBOURFRONT LRT PROJECT

LEGEND:
~~~~ BELOW GRADE
━━━ AT GRADE
◖━◗ L.R.T. PLATFORM AREAS

▲ A refurbished PCC car is seen leaving the Spadina Avenue terminus to turn on to Queens Quay on the first morning of operation.   *E.A. Wickson*

▼ The subway portal in the median strip of Queens Quay, with a PCC emerging after the underground run from Union Station.
                                                                    E.A. Wickson

▲ An eastbound car on Queens Quay, showing the raised reservation that is such a novelty in Toronto.   *E.A. Wickson*

▼ A view from the rebuilt railway bridge showing Spadina Avenue in the background. In a few years these tracks, at present used for depot journeys. will have a regular light rail service.
                                                                    E.A. Wickson

central reservation on the neighbourhood. Over the last 15 years Queens Quay has seen high-rise office, residential and hotel buildings and the original proposal for ballasted sleeper track was judged to be divisive. The TTC then came up with the less obtrusive Amsterdam-style reservation with rounded kerbs and tracks set in a concrete surface that can be crossed by pedestrians, and motor vehicles in an emergency. As TTC planner Juri Pill commented, "when it is built, everyone will wonder what all the fuss was about". Europeans will agree, but for Toronto this is an innovation.

The line was financed 75% by the Province of Ontario and 25% by Toronto's Metropolitan Council. The 5 metre high, 8.5 metre wide subway portion accounted for 50% of the cost. During excavation workers encountered waterlogged earth because of the high water table in the area, and had to use betonite consolidation for the side wall trenches. During construction the caissons bearing the central piers of the Toronto Terminal Railway bridge were exposed, and had to be collared with steel and concrete to provide lateral support. Also included in the project was the reconstruction of the Spadina bridge, widened from four to six lanes and incorporating the tram tracks for the service connection.

Thanks to the segregated right-of-way, trams can make a round trip on the line in 15 minutes. Service is provided from 06.08 (09.00 on Sundays) to 01.00 with cars every three minutes during Monday to Friday peak periods, every five minutes during daytime off-peak hours, and every eight minutes in the evenings (this level of service indicates the high standard that has been maintained in Toronto). This requires five cars at peaks and three at other times, carrying up to 5000 passengers/hour in each direction. Cars are drawn from the fleet of rebuilt PCCs (soon to total 23) authorised by the TTC in 1988. These all-electric cars of 1950–51 have been retained and upgraded because of an increased fleet requirement pending decisions on additional new cars

The Harbourfront LRT will be the last transit facility built in Toronto that is not fully accessible to the mobility impaired. The TTC is enthusiastic in its support of the provincial govern-

ment's new policy and funding commitment to fully-accessible public transport, and the needs of the elderly and disabled were taken into account in the design of the two underground stops on the line, at Union Station and Queens Quay–Ferry Docks (the latter due to open in early 1991, replacing temporary surface platforms). Accessibility to the cars requires the introduction of low-floor trams, and the purchase of this design is now a priority for the TTC following the recent authorisation of the Spadina LRT line.

As already mentioned, 800 m of the Spadina line already exists as service track to link the Harbourfront LRT with the TTC tramway system and its depots. The route was served by trams until October 1948, and some of the tracks have been retained since that time. Restoration of tram service has been delayed by TTC's insistence that for cost-effective operation the line must function as segregated LRT, and residents' and shopkeepers' fears that this would divide the community each side of one of Toronto's widest streets. Once again such arguments will seem strange to Europeans, but they required the plans to be subject to a detailed environmental assessment by a special consultative committee over a three-year period. This resulted in eventual agreement to an Amsterdam-style reservation, but required a commitment from the TTC to introduce low-floor cars for the opening of the line in 1996.

The CD$ 123 million 3.5 km project will link the Queens Quay end of Spadina Ave with Bloor St metro station, where there will be an underground loop (contributing CD$ 49.4 million to the cost). This cost does not include the purchase of the 16 LRVs needed to run the line. The TTC and local politicians have a preference for a 100% low-floor design, but the TTC is doubtful that a version compatible with the parameters of its existing network can be delivered by 1996, given the current prototype nature of this type of car. A final decision will need to be made by the end of 1992. These will be the first low-floor trams in North America, where hitherto the accessibility requirement has been met by lifts at one door on the vehicle, lifts or ramps at street stops to serve one door, or high platforms. No doubt the other operators will be watching the Toronto experience closely.

Thus after a period of uncertainty, the tramway is again expanding in Toronto, albeit under the new guise of light rail transit. Further extension of the Harbourfront line west to the Canadian National Exhibition could follow.

▲ A decorated PCC car led the opening procession of Toronto's Harbourfront light rail line on 22nd June 1990. 4500 is seen entering the Spadina loop at the west end of the line. *E.A. Wickson*

► The other end of the line is in subway to provide interchange with the heavy rapid transit system. PCC 4549 was the last new PCC car delivered to Toronto, in 1951, and was refurbished in 1989 with cosmetic restoration to original condition.

E.A. Wickson

The next generation -and the next

London Docklands Light Railway continues to expand with a new light rail extension eastwards towards the Royal Docks and Beckton.

To meet increased demand and provide additional capacity Hawker Siddeley Rail Projects and B.N., formerly La Brugeoise et Nivelles, have collaborated in supplying the new generation of 70 cars which will include:

- wider outside slidlng doors for easier access
- increased facilities for the mobility impaired
- improved fire rating for tunnel running
- ability to operate as multiple unit trains
- reduced interior and exterior noise levels
- enhanced passenger information system

BN are responsible for the vehicle design and production of mechanical parts. Hawker Siddeley Group will be supplying propulsion, braking, doors, heating and the automatic train operation equipment.

Hawker Siddeley Rail Projects will be responsible for project management of the UK scope of supply for this new European collaborative venture.

For further information on the 'next generation' Docklands car, please contact:

Hawker Siddeley Rail Projects Ltd.
PO Box 319, Foundry Lane, CHIPPENHAM, SN15 1EE
Telephone: (0249)443166, Telex: 445743,
Telefax: (0249) 443165

or

B.N.
Avenue Louise 65, 1050 BRUSSELS, Belgium
Telephone: 02-535-5511, Telex: 61736
Telefax: 02-539-1017

St Anne's Church, Limehouse

BOMBARDIER | **BN** | HAWKER SIDDELEY **RAIL PROJECTS**

LONDON DOCKLANDS
The DLR's Dash for Growth
by David Carter

A BACKGROUND TO DOCKLANDS

In 1981 the government formed the London Docklands Development Corporation (LDDC) to regenerate the Docklands, a vast half-derelict area of east London that had suffered from dock closures since the mid-1960s. The area was given Enterprise Zone status. Government money was to be used to 'pump-prime' the private sector into regenerating the area which covers the areas of Surrey Docks, Wapping, Poplar, the Isle of Dogs, the Royal Docks and Leamouth.

Funding for the original £77 million 12.1 km Docklands Light Railway (DLR) system came equally from the Department of the Environment and the Department of Transport. This government money was channelled through the LDDC and the Greater London Council respectively. With the abolition of the latter organisation soon afterwards, the Department of Transport money was diverted via London Regional Transport (LRT). The DLR is a wholly-owned subsidiary of LRT.

With the commitment from 1987 by Canadian multinational developers Olympia and York to build the £4 billion Canary Wharf – currently the world's largest commercial development – the whole scale and pace of Docklands development changed. In came both visions of a city of the future and the huge problem of assuring enough transport capacity to cope with demand.

Original plans envisaged 1m–1½ m square feet a year of new office space in the LDDC area till the mid-1990s; Canary Wharf will add 2 million square feet annually in 1991–96 alone. The related developments for retail and leisure at Port East and residential use at Heron Quays will increase passenger demand even more. In what is billed by the developers as 'London's third business district', 50 000 people will work at Canary Wharf, with a further 80 000 working elsewhere in the Isle of Dogs/ Leamouth area. The current commercial property recession will probably delay this growth. Early in the next century 200 000 people could be working in the Docklands area.

The recession has left the LDDC unable to sell much land for development, its only source of funds at a time when it is committed to building infrastructure. Resignations from the corporation have added to the uncertain environment in which the DLR finds itself.

Transport has become the most pressing issue in Docklands. From the almost completely publicly-funded DLR and roads network to the Jubilee Line extension with its greater private sector involvement, there is still a race against time to prevent the Docklands dream becoming a nightmare.

THE EXISTING SYSTEM

The original network centres on Poplar with lines northwards to Stratford, south to Island Gardens and west to Tower Gateway. The DLR mostly uses old British Rail alignments and features both sharp bends and steep gradients. Only the section crossing the docks is entirely new. The lines converge at the Delta Junction which lies between Poplar, West India Quay and Westferry stations.

With normally two LRVs being maintained at any one time at the Poplar maintenance depot, up to nine out of the original 11 can be used to offer Tower Gateway–Island Gardens and Stratford–Island Gardens services. These six-axle articulated vehicles, designated P86, have given reasonable service and have proved popular with passengers. The LRVs are automatic and so an excellent view is afforded, from the front window, of both the railway and the impressive Docklands townscape. On visiting the DLR, one often has to rush for the front seats to beat the camera-clicking German, American and Japanese tourists! Regular passengers and tourists alike welcome the system's cleanliness. In contrast to the London Underground, graffiti vandalism is rare and only one station on the network suffers regularly from more conventional vandalism. The distinctive 'train captains' are free to check tickets, help passengers, operate the doors and drive the trains if the Automatic Train Operation (ATO) system fails.

The GEC-Alsthom signalling is controlled from the control room at the Operations and Maintenance centre at Poplar. It

►Brand new BREL-built cars stand alongside Poplar depot, with Nos. 12 and 17 in the foreground. They were awaiting the addition of equipment to enable them to run successfully as two-car units, as well as other features. Coupling problems have meant that, even at the time of writing, not all the units have been accepted for service. The date is 26th March 1990.   *Peter Fox*

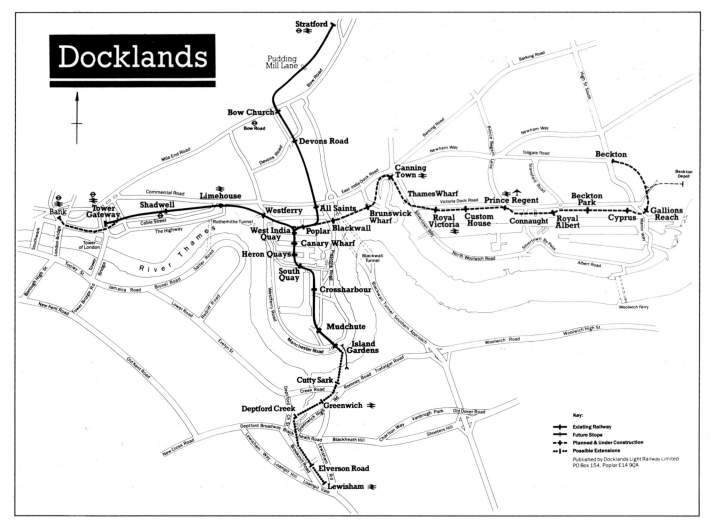

Route map of the Docklands Light Railway system, adapted to include the latest changes. The Lewisham extension passes under the River Thames to the west of the Greenwich Foot Tunnel. On the Beckton extension, London City Airport lies on the spit of land to the south of Royal Albert, Beckton Park and Cyprus stations.

operates with fixed blocks based on solid-state interlockings (SSI). Automatic Train Supervision (ATS) operates interactively with Automatic Train Protection (ATP) and ATO. The ATP has overriding rule over the others and over human intervention. As on the systems being experimentally installed on BR's London Paddington–Bristol line and Chiltern Lines, ATP is designed to stop any train going too fast for line conditions or entering a section occupied by another train. The control room supervisor can control ATS, ATP and ATO. ATS can also monitor the service to correct delays and regulate headways without any manual intervention; it does this by selecting, from available acceleration, speed and braking profiles (and taking into account local speed restrictions, gradients, etc.), the type of inter-station performance.

The 11 original LRVs and new-build vehicles are powered from a 750 V dc third rail. Bottom-running shoegear interfaces with the third rail, made from an aluminium/stainless steel extrusion. For safety reasons the third rail is shrouded by plastic on all sides except the running surface which is therefore protected from the elements. Track workers are also more protected when having to step over the live third rail, a relatively rare occurrence. In contrast to the more usual methods of maintaining (albeit variable) pressure between shoe and rail – gravity and by the use of springs – constant pressure is maintained on the DLR current collection system by means of 'air-on' pneumatics. The system has proved successful and a similar, but simpler bottom-running current collection system is used on Singapore's new MRT system. Brecknell, Willis Ltd. have supplied both. The LRVs offer a maximum speed of 80 km/h and can accommodate up to 220 passengers, 84 of

these seated. The 7½-minute headways used on the existing system equates to a maximum of 2 500–3 000 passengers per hour.

The project found favour in 1982 with passenger estimates of 11 500 per day during its first year. Within months of opening the system was actually carrying twice that figure. By 1990, 33 000 passengers a day were being carried – on a network forecast to carry a maximum that year of only 20 000 a day and 22 000 by 1992.

An eight-fold increase in the DLR's capacity is underway, to be completed in 1992, with the most dramatic increases occurring between Bank/Tower Gateway and Crossharbour. The station at Crossharbour is at the southern edge of the most intensive commercial development and so is a good point to terminate and turn around most services from the City. By 1992 some services from Stratford will also terminate at Crossharbour.

Island Gardens is not neglected, however, with an expansion of services in 1992 when the final batch of new Belgian-built cars are delivered. With the expansion of capacity and extensions to the system to be discussed shortly, the DLR will be able to handle up to 15 000 passengers an hour from that key year. The busiest stretch of line will be Bank/Tower Gateway–Westferry, with the stretch south to Crossharbour almost as busy.

By the late 1990s, the Lewisham extension (discussed at the end of this article) will entail the DLR carrying more than 40 000 passengers per hour into the Isle of Dogs. The transformation from the original railway will have been truly remarkable.

▲Operators at work inside the DLR control room at Poplar depot on 9th January 1991. *Brian Morrison*

► Low evening sunlight at Canary Wharf in October 1990. Until the station's planned opening in April 1991, trains run through the station without stopping. The original centre tracks have been removed for station building to take place.
Marysha Alwan/DLR

◄ An aerial view of the Canary Wharf complex on 18th June 1990. Further away is West India Quay station and, to the right of the Delta Junction, Poplar station and depot. The tracks to the left go to Tower Gateway.
Chorley and Handford Ltd.

EXPANSION OF DOCKLANDS CAPACITY

Platform Lengthening. All platforms, except those at Mudchute and Island Gardens, have been lengthened to accommodate two-car trains. However, there is no intention of running the two-car trains south of Crossharbour until the DLR's Lewisham extension is built. Stratford–Island Gardens services will therefore continue to be operated by single cars, probably of P86 stock, with some new vehicles supplementing the service in 1992. At Tower Gateway, concourse improvements have accompanied platform lengthenings to smooth passenger flows; the changes include a new east-end exit staircase to Mansell Street.

New Stations. Canary Wharf will be served from April 1991 by a station with three tracks and six platforms, all beneath a high glazed arched roof, so matching its gradiose surroundings. Olympia and York have contributed £25 million towards the station's construction. The station's two outer lines will probably serve through services to Crossharbour/Island Gardens/ Lewisham. The centre track will mainly cater for terminating services. The station is designed for maximum one-way flows of 20 000 passengers an hour, implying eventual three-car trains running every two minutes, the system's normal minimum headway. The headway can, incidentally be reduced to 90 seconds when delays are being corrected. The new Canary Wharf station will be just a nine-minute journey from the 'old' City. The DLR station's capacity will be supplemented by the late 1990s by the adjacent Jubilee Line station, to be built as part of the line's £1 billion extension from central London out to Docklands and Stratford.

There is the possibility of a new station at Leman Street near the junction of the new Bank lines just east of Tower Gateway. A new station at Pudding Mill Lane between Bow Church and Stratford should be in service by 1995 but a new station between All Saints and Devons Road at Carmen Street is now unlikely in the near future.

New Trackwork. A crossing loop has been installed at Pudding Mill Lane. Crossharbour station's southern end has been re-modelled to include a reversing and storage track for trains terminating there. A Bill is also now making its way through Parliament which would add two more tracks between the Delta Junction at Poplar and Canary Wharf, involving the closure of West India Quay station for several months from

Summer 1991.

New Trains. The ten BREL-built P89 cars were delivered in 1989 and 1990 and are now all in passenger-carrying operation. In the longer term they will probably form five 2-car trains and will not operate with P86 stock. Tests are currently being undertaken with a two-car train formed of BREL vehicles. The new cars feature programmable Liquid Crystal Display destination boards which show the route and terminus both inside and outside both ends of the vehicle; these LCD displays are also being retro-fitted to P86 vehicles. The new P89 cars are able to run into the Bank extension tunnel from the start as they meet all fire requirements for such operations.

Just over half of the 70 vehicles also being delivered from BN Constructions from January 1991 onwards will go towards increasing frequency and therefore capacity on the present network and on services to Bank. The rest will operate Beckton services from 1992. The BN vehicles should be delivered at the rate of two a week.

▲ The first of the BN B90 stock vehicles built for the DLR is seen on the company's test track in Brugge. No. 22 will have the pantograph removed before the unit's delivery to Poplar at the end of January 1991. The special shoegear, new sliding doors, and end door for emergency use can be seen. *DLR*

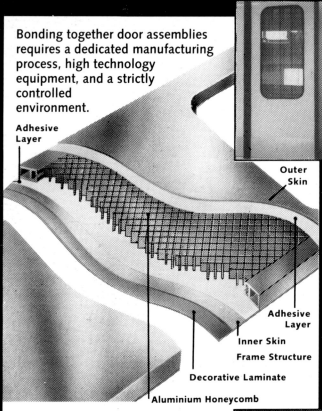

▲ The BREL cars' doors are being adapted to improve clearance from passengers (and their bags). The P86 cars' doors have not been modified yet, hence the warning sticker top left. The BREL cars will work to Bank station, as will BN-built cars (equipped with sliding doors). A DLR train captain operates the overhead console of her train at Poplar on 7th January 1991. *Brian Morrison*

▼ A view from the tunnel mouth at Royal Mint Street on the Bank extension. Note the walkway on the right. The date is 1st November 1990. *Brian Morrison*

▶A diesel shunter with match wagon-stands on the eastbound ('Down') track out of the Bank tunnel on 1st November 1990. On the 'Up' track is a pair of road/rail engineers' vehicles. Behind this severely-graded new track lies the DLR/BR viaduct to Tower Gateway and Fenchurch Street stations respectively.
Brian Morrison

▼The breakthrough of the tunnel at Bank station on 1st November 1990.   *Brian Morrison*

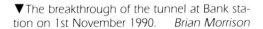

THE BANK EXTENSION

The present western terminus of the DLR is Tower Gateway on the eastern fringe of the City of London, itself still a remarkably concentrated commercial area. This will be largely replaced by a new underground DLR station at Bank, 42 m beneath King William Street in the heart of the City.

The 1.5 km extension leaves the elevated track section just south-east of Tower Gateway station at Leman Street, the possible site for a new station. Descending rapidly it enters two separate single track tunnels at Royal Mint Street. The tunnel follows the course of the local road network where possible to avoid any problems arising from boring below foundations. The lines run deep underground below Tower Hill, along Byward Street, Great Tower Street and Eastcheap.

The Bank extension is steeply-graded, including one 300 m stretch of 6%. This compares with a maximum of 4.3% elsewhere on the system and under 3% on the British Rail network.

Each single track tunnel is 4.9 m in diameter allowing room each side of the track for a continuous walkway, or narrow platform, to be used by passengers in emergencies. The two bores diverge slightly and their diameters increase to 7 m for the station itself. Each track is signalled for bi-directional working.

Bank station's platforms are 85 m long, enough to accommodate three-car trains eventually. Between the two platforms is a concourse with escalators at each end. At the northern end, escalators and a lift provide connections with the nearby Northern Line, and, a longer walk away, the Central Line and BR's Waterloo and City line. At the southern end, the DLR will be connected to the Circle and District lines at Monument. It was intended originally to rename the whole complex of lines and stations as 'Bank' but the original divisions are now to be maintained, to prevent confusion between stations in emergen-

cies. A total of 500 m of new subways has been built plus five new escalator flights and a new lift shaft. The construction of the DLR's new Bank station is being supplemented by improvements at some of London Underground's stations, escalators and passageways at Bank. Network SouthEast's Waterloo and City Line is also being improved at last and the whole area resembles the proverbial bomb site.

In all, the Bank extension project has cost some £160 million with about £68 million of this being provided by Canary Wharf developers Olympia & York. Edmund Nuttall is the main contractor.

Beyond the station itself, the two bores converge by means of a step-plate junction to a single overrun tunnel running as far as the ventilation shaft at Lothbury, beneath Princes Street. The overrun allows incoming (westbound) trains to cross over to the outgoing (eastbound) track.

There have been delays in construction of the Bank extension caused by unforeseen ground conditions. Subsidence, causing cracks to appear in Mansion House, slowed work for several months, during which a protracted set of legal negotiations were held between Nuttall, Maunsell, the DLR Board and the Corporation of London. Public service is expected to start in July 1991, using one track initially.

The future of Tower Gateway is uncertain after the Bank extension opens. For the time being, apart from the concourse improvements mentioned, congestion has been eased by the provision of a 'lay-over' unit in the station. Unlike when the system first opened, the new operation enables boarding to take place before the arrival of the next incoming service. Trains still have to negotiate the station's single-track 'throat', however. Tower Gateway will probably be retained for peak-hour working, as a reserve terminus and for emergency operation.

◄ The plethora of tunnels beneath Bank and Monument is shown in this DLR illustration. The depth of the DLR's Bank extension can be seen.

▼Diagram showing the new layout near the Delta Junction.   *DLR*

►An aerial view of the Beckton extension, with Royal Albert, Beckton Park, Cyprus, and Gallions Reach (in the distance) stations under construction. London City Airport is on the right. The date is 9th August 1990.   *DLR*

►▼The new West India Quay Down Viaduct takes shape alongside the existing North Quay Viaduct.   *DLR*

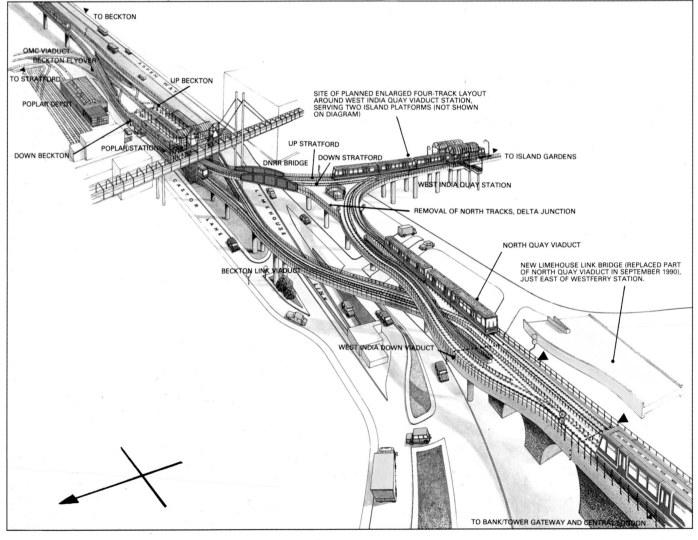

THE BECKTON EXTENSION

The vast expanses of Leamouth and the Royal Docks should be connected to the existing system by the end of 1992. These areas are widely-regarded as two of the best remaining development sites in Britain. The first £20 million phase of the £240 million extension to Beckton involves the remodelling of Delta Junction and the expansion of the adjacent station at Poplar. The station is being rebuilt from a three-track twin-island layout to a four-track twin-island layout. Balfour Beatty is managing contract No. 1 which extends roughly 1 km either side of Poplar station. The new layout is far more complicated than the previous one and rather resembles a big dipper. For Bank/Tower Gateway–Canary Wharf/Island Gardens passengers their route will remain broadly familiar. For passengers travelling from Bank/Tower Gateway to Beckton, they will traverse the new Limehouse Link Bridge and then the Beckton Link Viaduct which runs below the lofty down West India Viaduct which supports the line to Island Gardens. They will pass close by the well-known blue bridge (which carries Stratford–Island Gardens services over the road once labelled the Docklands Northern Relief Road) and into platform one at Poplar. Platforms two and three will be served by Stratford–Island Gardens services, platform four by Beckton–Bank/Tower Gateway services.

This platform arrangement will therefore provide easy cross-platform connections for people making journeys from Stratford to Bank/Tower Gateway and from Beckton to the Isle of Dogs. As well as the main entrance in Castor Lane, overhead footpaths are planned at Poplar linking the station with neighbouring developments and with Poplar High Street.

From Poplar, the Stratford lines and single southern access line to the Operations and Maintenance centre run below a new viaduct carrying the Beckton lines – the 'OMC flyover'.

When the junctions for the Beckton extension are completed, the lines on the north side of the original Delta Junction will be removed.

The 7.5 km extension will feature 11 new stations, with a further two being considered. Beckton contract No. 2 is the responsibility of Mowlem and Taylor Woodrow. The DLR project is financed fully by the LDDC, by borrowing and from land sales.

Construction of the line from Poplar to Beckton is proceeding according to plan, but delays have occurred due to problems with the setting of concrete on the very hot days of July, when temperatures exceeded 38°. One of the structures in the Connaught area has had to be recast, but it is confidently anticipated that the whole scheme will be finished on schedule.

Stations at Royal Albert, Beckton Park and Cyprus were built early as part of the spine road upgrading schemes. The latter two are sub-surface stations located in road roundabouts and are designed from the outset to accommodate three-car trains; their extension after the road is completed would be very costly and difficult. It is sad to see that early indications are the certain stations on the Beckton extension will suffer from graffiti vandalism. Hopefully, it will be cleaned off promptly each time it appears until the offenders are caught or tire of trying.

Minimum curve radii will be greater than on the existing system because the new line follows a more open alignment. The Beckton line will comprise roughly equal amounts of sub-surface, ground-level and elevated track and, as elsewhere, be generally slab-tracked on viaducts and ballasted on the level and in underpasses.

A new maintenance depot at Beckton is also being built, there being single-line access from both up and down lines. Although Poplar Operations and Maintenance centre is being expanded to take up 31 cars, the Beckton depot will become the main maintenance facility on the DLR system. Poplar depot will handle some routine inspections and effect any short-term repairs.

When the DLR system first opened, traction power was provided from a single substation at Poplar. With the fleet increasing in size from 11 to 91 cars before 1992 new substations will be added. They will be spread throughout the system at Royal Mint Street, Crossharbour, Bow Church and Beckton.

The Beckton extension will be served by 34 out of the 70 BN cars. The LDDC is funding 28 of these, LRT the other six. BN are responsible for the vehicle design and production of mechanical parts with Chippenham-based Hawker Siddeley supplying electrical sub-systems. The vehicles will have sliding instead of inward-folding plug doors, no doubt to the relief of passengers. Deans Powered Doors Ltd. of Humberside is supplying the new doors. Design capacity is for 260 passengers, the vast majority standing. The BN cars will have connections between them for staff, only to be used when a train is stationary. If a two-car train fails, the train captain will need to get to the front of the leading car to drive manually.

The first ten BN trains – designated B90 – are nearing completion at Brugge. The other 60 will be a mixture of B90 and B92 stock, the former, like P86 and P89 vehicles, responding to the existing GEC signalling system, the latter to 'SEL-TRAC' signalling. The £26.4 million contract for the installation and commissioning of Alcatel's SELTRAC2 'moving block' system was awarded in October 1990 but precise phasing of signalling changes is unclear. The Beckton extension will operate under SELTRAC2 from the start, with probable GEC/SELTRAC2 dual-fitting of vehicles and track elsewhere until the complete transition of the entire DLR to SELTRAC2 is complete. A minimum headway of 60 seconds is claimed by Alcatel.

The SELTRAC2 system is 'transmission based' which monitors the performance of each train and interracts, by transmission, in a similar fashion to the existing signalling system, with computers in the control centre; there are three levels of computer operation in the hierarchy.

THE DLR'S CONNECTIONS TO LONDON CITY AIRPORT

Britain's newest airport was opened in January 1988 and is served by STOL De Havilland DASH 7 aircraft operating short-haul international flights. Destinations are limited due to the type's 400-mile maximum range. In 1990 London City Airport served up to 240 000 passengers, an increase of 61% on the figure for its first year of operation.

Despite its proximity to the City and short check-in times, a lack of good roads and railways to the airport has hindered its growth.Currently, 80% of air passengers reach the airport by car or taxi, 12–15% by riverbus and 5% via the North London Line and/or foot.

Once the DLR's Beckton extension opens there is great scope to attract much existing and new traffic to the airport. The Charing Cross–London City Airport Pier riverbus is fast, taking only 20 minutes, but only runs hourly. The local road network is being upgraded at vast expense but traffic congestion makes reliability more of a problem. BR's North London Line is better than it was (with newer rolling stock and a clearer management structure) but it remains a poor relation on the Network SouthEast system; it does not serve the City and the nearest station at Silvertown station is a circuitous walk from

the airport terminal. The re-siting of this station a few hundred metres to the east – to be closer to the airport – has been mooted.

From 1993 to 1996 it is planned that buses will link the airport with the DLR at Prince Regent. After that the connection will be made further away at Canning Town, also one of the stations on the Jubilee Line extension. A passenger lounge is to be built at Canning Town purely for airport passengers. This is to introduce the 'airport culture' to a passenger's journey at an early stage.

Passenger flow forecasts for the Beckton extension will be increased if London City Airport is given authority to extend its runway and accept aircraft like the BAe 146 with its 1000-mile range. This relatively quiet jet could serve destinations as far away as Lisboa, Roma, Berlin and Stockholm. A decision is expected late in 1991.

▲ The viaduct for the Beckton extension between Gallions Reach and the Beckton terminus is seen under construction on 6th January 1991. The opening of the DLR to this area, plus building of the proposed East London River Crossing nearby (to link the A2 with an upgraded A13), should greatly improve accessibility.
Brian Morrison

THE LEWISHAM EXTENSION

In one of his last acts as secretary of state for transport, Cecil Parkinson agreed on 20th November 1990 to a private Parliamentary Bill being introduced in Parliament seeking powers to construct the 4 km double track Island Gardens–Lewisham extension of the DLR. The Bill is sponsored by London Transport and will allow them to let a concession to a private sector company to build and run the £130 million extension. If approved by Parliament, the extension could be in operation by 1995. The Isle of Dogs will then have rail access from all directions.

Mudchute and Island Gardens stations will be re-sited slightly to the east in the current plans to ensure a relatively easy gradient from the existing viaduct to the 1 km tunnel under the River Thames. This will run parallel to the existing Greenwich foot tunnel. South of the river there will be stations at Cutty Sark (underground), Greenwich, Deptford Bridge (elevated), Elverson Road and Lewisham (elevated), although some details are likely to change before construction starts. The new station at Lewisham will be chosen to be a short walk from the town centre, the bus station and BR's station, possibly all by covered walkways.

Trains south of the river would be owned privately and pay a toll when using lines north of the river to Bank/Tower Gateway and Stratford. The DLR would have to pay tolls when its trains entered the private line south of the Thames. The Department of Transport indicated that the private operator would probably "sub-contract some aspect of the operation of the railway to the DLR or other qualified railway operator."

By December 1990, several developers had expressed interest in contributing to the extension, which has come out well in cost-benefit analyses compared with other major rail projects in London. With the Deptford area having been identified by the government as an inner-city renewal priority area, work has started on redeveloping a large area of the riverside between Greenwich Town and Deptford Creek. Lewisham town centre (the largest such centre in inner London) and the more westerly parts of the 12 km of riverfront between Greenwich, Woolwich and Thamesmead are also likely to benefit economically from the new cross-river link.

The Lewisham extension will allow a direct link via Docklands between north-east and south-east London by using BR Network SouthEast services at Stratford, Greenwich and Lewisham. Similarly, DLR's Limehouse station is close to BR's, itself situated on the London Fenchurch Street–Southend Central line. Journey times between Lewisham and Canary Wharf or between Lewisham and Stratford could be as little as a third of those via BR's London Bridge or via the BR-Underground connection at New Cross.

A maximum flow of 8 800 passengers an hour is expected for the extension on opening. This equates with 20 two-car trains per hour per route with a three-minute headway. This could later be increased to 12 000 passengers an hour with two-minute headways, and 18 000–20 000 with three-car trains.

On a general planning note, the north-south axis of the Lewisham–Canary Wharf–Stratford section of the DLR should compliment both the DLR's Bank/Tower Gateway–Beckton section and London Underground's Jubilee Line which both run in an east-west corridor.

Residents and commuters from Lewisham, Deptford and Greenwich will have new choice in how to reach all three London business districts more easily: Canary Wharf; the City; and the West End by changing at Canary Wharf on to the Jubilee Line. Despite continuing arguments about the Jubilee Line's precise route between Canary Wharf and Canning Town, the huge capacity of the Underground (100 000 passengers an hour in each direction) can only serve to limit overcrowding at peak times for certain DLR passengers – for instance for those travelling from Lewisham to Bank.

Off-peak patronage is likely to be healthy, partly due to the popularity of Greenwich town and park by tourists. 1.5 million tourists a year visit Greenwich already, despite awkward public transport links. The Lewisham extension could account for 17 million cross-river journeys a year when both peak and off-peak travel are considered.

Lewisham and Greenwich councils have both offered financial support to encourage a decision on the extension. Both councils have seen the DLR as a vital element in the regeneration of their areas. With local government finance so tight at the moment, any support to a private company or consortium will probably be in the form of land deals.

OTHER EXTENSIONS

Various extensions to the DLR have been suggested, officially and unofficially, including Beckton–Barking and Stratford–Walthamstow. Practically all planning work is currently devoted to the Lewisham extension, however.

CONCLUSION

For all the talk of gloom, the transport infrastructure in Docklands is taking shape. £3 billion is being spent supporting the £8 billion of private investment in Docklands committed since 1981. The £500 million upgrading and expansion of the DLR will be an essential part of this support.

ACKNOWLEDGEMENTS

Brecknell, Willis & Co. Ltd.
Docklands Light Railway Ltd. (special thanks to Robin Pulford and Marysha Alwan)
Greenwich Borough Council
Lewisham Borough Council
London City Airport
London Docklands Development Corporation
London Regional Transport
Olympia & York

▲Bow Church station on 16th February 1990 shows the new platform extensions, sealed off at the time by barriers. Bow Church DLR station is a short walk away from the Underground's station at Bow Road on the District Line.   *Brian Morrison*

A DLR AND DOCKLANDS DIARY

07/81	The LDDC is created, its aim to redevelop the docks in 10 years.
10/82	The government authorises the construction of the DLR.
08/84	London Regional Transport awards the main DLR construction contract to the GEC-Mowlem Railway Group.
12/84	Construction of the DLR starts.
12/86	The DLR's Bank extension receives Royal Assent.
03/87	Government support for the Beckton extension is announced.
07/87	The DLR is officially opened by the Queen.
08/87	The new system opens to the public.
03/88	Work starts on the £150 million Bank extension, about a half of the cost being met by Olympia & York. BREL Ltd. wins a contract for 10 new trains.
02/89	BN of Belgium wins a contract for 10 new trains.
06/89	The £1 billion Jubilee Line extension to Docklands is authorised.
07/89	The £240 million Beckton extension receives Royal Assent. The BN order is increased to 44 cars.
02/90	Work officially starts on construction of the Beckton extension.
09/90	A new 80 metre bridge between Westferry and West India Quay/Poplar replaces the original six-arch North Quay viaduct. This will enable the new Limehouse Link (an underground road linking Wapping with the Isle of Dogs) to be built immediately beneath the railway without disruption in services. The new bridge will carry the Westferry emergency crossover as well as the main lines.
10/90	BN win a £20 million order for 26 more vehicles for an enhanced Stratford–Island Gardens service from 1992. This brings to 70 the number of new vehicles being built by BN.
11/90	Hoisting the stainless steel pyramid cap to its place on top of the 49-storey, 800 ft tower of Canary Wharf, symbolically marks the completion of its external structure. The government approves the deposit of a Private Bill to allow the private sector to extend the DLR from Island Gardens to Lewisham. Tunnel boring of the Bank extension is completed.
01/91	First BN cars arrive.
03/91	First Reading of Lewisham Bill expected.
04/91	Canary Wharf station is scheduled to open. This could be deferred to June or July, however.
06/91	Work starts on the expansion of the layout at West India Quay station. Eventually, four tracks will lead south where they will converge to three at Canary Wharf.
07/91	Bank extension phase 1 (single track to Bank) is scheduled to open, services operating every eight minutes.
12/91	Testing of SELTRAC2 signalling system starts on Beckton extension.
03/92	Bank extension phase 2 (double track to Bank) is scheduled to open.
11/92	Delivery of the first batch of 44 BN cars is completed.
12/92	Beckton extension is scheduled to open.
1993	Possible withdrawal of original P86 cars.
1995	Lewisham extension opens.

WORLD LIST
Urban Tramway and Light Rail Systems, 1990

by Michael Taplin

▲ A three-car set of Tatra T5 trams on the 1990 extension of express tramway route 1 along Hungaria korut to Thököly ut in Budapest which uses the typical east European concrete track panels with U-cross section rails laid in rubber-lined channel.
N. Griffiths

◀ Japanese tramways continue to hold their own amid increasingly chaotic traffic conditions, exemplified by this scene in Okayama. The tram is one of many new examples purchased by Japanese systems in recent years. *S. Turnbull*

▼ Two trains on San Diego's expanding light rail network pass in front of the Santa Fe station on the Bayside line opened in 1990. *J. Wolinsky*

Key: * Systems built new since 1985.
 § Systems extending or extended recently, including subway construction.
 † Systems with no light rail features.
 (T) Heritage tramway operated primarily for tourist purposes.

Systems in italics are steel wheel, automated, fully-segregated lines.

ARGENTINA

Buenos Aires*.

AUSTRALIA

Adelaide, Bendigo(T), Melbourne§.

AUSTRIA

Gmunden, Graz, Innsbruck, Linz§, Wien (Vienna)§.

BELGIUM

Antwerpen§, Bruxelles/Brussel (Brussels)§, Charleroi§, Gent§, Oostende.

BRAZIL

Campos do Jordao, Rio de Janeiro* (also T).

BULGARIA

Sofia§.

CANADA

Calgary*, Edmonton*, Toronto§, *Vancouver**.

CHINA

Anshan, Changchun, Dalian.

CZECHOSLOVAKIA

Bratislava§, Brno§, Kosice, Liberec, Most, Olomouc, Ostrava, Plzen§, Praha (Prague)§, Teplice-Trencianska.

EGYPT

El Qahira (Cairo)§, Helwan*, Iskandariyah (Alexandria), Masr-el-Gedida (Heliopolis).

FINLAND

Helsinki§.

FRANCE

Grenoble*, Lille, Marseille, Nantes*, St Etienne§.

GERMANY

Augsburg§, Bad Schandau(T), Berlin (East)§, Bielefeld§, Bochum-Gelsenkirchen§, Bonn, Brandenburg§, Braunschweig§, Bremen, Chemnitz§, Cottbus§, Darmstadt, Dessau§, Dortmund§, Dresden§, Duisburg§, Düsseldorf§, Erfurt§, Essen§, Frankfurt/Main§, Frankfurt/Oder§, Freiburg/Breisgau§, Gera§, Gotha, Görlitz§, Halberstadt†, Halle§, Hannover§, Heidelburg§, Jena§, Karlsruhe§, Kassel§, Köln (Cologne)§, Krefeld§, Leipzig, Ludwigshafen, Magdeburg, Mainz§, Mannheim, Mülheim/Ruhr§, München (Munich), Naumburg†, Nordhausen†, Nürnberg, Plauen§, Potsdam§, Rostock§, Schöneiche, Schwerin§, Strausberg, Stuttgart§, Ulm, Woltersdorf†, Würzburg§, Zwickau§.

Note: The two Germanys were combined as one country on 3rd October 1990. Chemnitz gained its former name from Karl-Marx-Stadt.

HONG KONG

Hong Kong†, Tuen Men*.

▶ The Mexican city of Guadalajara has joined the light rail club recently with a system designed and procured by Germany's Light Rail Transit Consultants. The locally-built cars are similar to the Duewag U2 design and feature Siemens electrical equipment.   *S. J. Morgan*

HUNGARY
Budapest§, Debrecen†, Miskolc†, Szeged†.

INDIA
Calcutta§.

ITALY
Genova*, Milano§, Napoli§, Roma§, Torino§.

JAPAN
Enoshima, Fukui, Gifu, Hakodate, Hiroshima, Kagoshima, Kitakyushu, Kochi, Kuamamonto, Kyoto, Matsuyama, Nagasaki, Okayama, Osaka, Sapporo, Takaoka, Tokyo, Toyama, Toyohashi.

MEXICO
Guadalajara*, Mexico City§.

NETHERLANDS
Amsterdam§, Den Haag (The Hague)§, Rotterdam§, Utrecht*.

NORWAY
Oslo, Trondheim.

PARAGUAY
Asuncion†.

PHILIPPINES
Manila*.

POLAND
Bydgoszcz§, Czestochowa, Elblag§, Gdansk (Danzig)§, Grudziadz, Katowice, Krakow, Lodz, Poznan, Szczecin (Stettin), Torun§, Warszawa (Warsaw)§, Wroclaw (Breslau).

PORTUGAL
Lisboa†, Porto†.

ROMANIA
Arad§, Braila, Brasov*, Bucuresti§, Cluj*, Constanta*, Craiova*, Galati§, Iasi§, Oradea§, Ploeisti*, Resita*, Sibiu†, Timisoara§.

SPAIN
Barcelona(T), Soller(T), Valencia*.

SWEDEN
Göteborg (Gothenburg)§, Lidingö, Norrköping§, Stockholm.

SWITZERLAND
Basel§, Bern, Bex†, Genève§, Neuchâtel, Zürich§.

TUNISIA
Tunis*.

TURKEY
Istanbul*.

UNITED KINGDOM
Blackpool, Douglas(T), *London**, Newcastle-upon-Tyne*.

UNITED STATES
Boston, Buffalo*, Cleveland, Dallas(T), *Detroit** (also T), Fort Worth, Galveston(T), Los Angeles*, Newark, New Orleans (also T), Philadelphia, Pittsburgh§, Portland*, Sacramento*, San Diego*, San Francisco§, San Jose*, Seattle(T).

USSR
(§† information not available).

Achinsk, Alma Ata, Angarsk, Arkhangelsk, Astrakhan, Avdeyevka, Baku, Barnaul, Biysk, Chelyabinsk, Cherepovets, Daugavpils, Dneprodzerzhinsk, Dnepropetrovsk, Donetsk, Druzhkovka, Dzerzhinsk, Gorki, Gorlovka, Grozniy, Irkutsk, Ivanovo, Kalinin, Kaliningrad,

▲ Oslo, Norway, is another Scandanavian capital which has taken delivery of new trams recently. Their six-axle cars are built by local firm Stroemmen under Duewag licence.
                                                                    S. Mohn

▼ Melbourne is putting large numbers of six-axle trams into service, built by ABB subsidiary Comeng. However arguments continue to rage in the city about the feasibility of one-man operation and a ticket system that would help this work.   *S. Turnbull*

Karaganda, Karpinsk, Kazan, Kemerovo, Khabarovsk, Kharkov, Kiev, Kolomna, Komsomolsk, Konotop, Konstantinovka, Kramatorsk, Krasnoarmeisk*, Krasnodar, Krasnoturinsk, Krasnoyarsk, Krivoy Rog, Kuibyshev, Kursk, Kuznetsk, Leningrad, Liepaya, Lipetsk, Lvov, Magnitogorsk, Makeyevka, Minsk, Molotzhnoye, Moskva (Moscow), Mosyr*, Naberezhnye-Chelny, Nikolayev, Nishnikamensk, Nishni Tagil, Noginsk, Novocherkassk, Novopolotsk, Novosibirsk, Novotroisk, Odessa, Omsk, Orzhonikidze, Orel, Orsk, Ossinniki, Pavlodar, Perm, Prokopyevsk, Pyatigorsk, Riga, Rostov-na-Donu, Ryazan, Salavat, Saratov, Shakhty, Shushenskoye, Smolensk, Stakhanov, Stary Oskol*, Sumgait, Sverdlovsk, Taganrog, Tallinn, Tashkent, Tbilisi, Termitau, Tomsk, Tula, Ufa, Ulan Ude, Ulyanovsk, Ussolye-Sibiriskoye, Ust-Ilimsk*, Ustinov, Ust-Kamenogorsk, Vinnitsa, Vitebsk, Vladivostock, Volgograd, Volzhskiy, Volchansk, Voronezh, Voroshilovgrad, Yaroslavl, Yenakievo, Yerevan, Yevpatoria, Zaporozhye, Zhdanov, Zhitomir, Zlatoust.

YUGOSLAVIA

Beograd§, Osijek§, Sarajevo, Zagreb§.

SYSTEMS UNDER CONSTRUCTION

BRAZIL: Campinas, Salvador.
FRANCE: Paris, Reims, Strasbourg.
MEXICO: Monterrey.
ROMANIA: Botosani.
SWEDEN: Stockholm (T).
SWITZERLAND: Lausanne.
TURKEY: Konya.
UK: Manchester, Sheffield.
USA: Baltimore, Dallas, Memphis (T), St Louis.
USSR: Togliatti.

SYSTEMS AUTHORISED

BRAZIL: Goiana, Teresina, Belo Horizonte.
CZECHOSLOVAKIA: Chomutov.
FRANCE: Rouen.
MALAYSIA: Kuala Lumpur.
UK: Birmingham, Bristol.
USA: Denver, Houston, Minneapolis, Jersey City.

SYSTEMS PLANNED

These include:

ARGENTINA: Cordoba.
AUSTRALIA: Sydney.
AUSTRIA: Salzburg.
BRAZIL: Brasilia.
COLOMBIA: Bogota.
FRANCE: Orleans.
ITALY: Bologna, Firenze.
MEXICO: Tijuana.
NEW ZEALAND: Auckland.
SPAIN: Barcelona.
UK: Cleveland, Edinburgh, London (Croydon), Nottingham, Portsmouth (Fareham).
USA: Chicago, Indianapolis, Norfolk, Phoenix, Seattle, Washington.

▲▲◄ The Genova light metro, opened in 1990, makes use of a tunnel built for the former tramway system to find an alignment between Certosa and Brin. Further sections are to be built on segregated alignment. *M. Moerland*

▲◄ The last of 47 Tatra KT8 trams delivered to Praha, Prague) in 1987–90. Tatra are hoping to demonstrate this design of car in western Europe. *M.R. Taplin*

◄ The future of China's three tramway systems is unclear, although some modernisation has taken place, and light rail consultants have been called in. Dalian is the busiest system, with its fleet of home-built articulated cars. *G. P. Warren*